Inward, Outward, Onward, Upward

American Alliance of Museums

The American Alliance of Museums has been bringing museums together since 1906, helping to develop standards and best practices, gathering and sharing knowledge, and providing advocacy on issues of concern to the entire museum community. Representing more than 35,000 individual museum professionals and volunteers, institutions, and corporate partners serving the museum field, the Alliance stands for the broad scope of the museum community.

The American Alliance of Museums' mission is to champion museums and nurture excellence in partnership with its members and allies.

Books published by AAM further the Alliance's mission to make standards and best practices for the broad museum community widely available.

American
Alliance of
Museums

Inward, Outward, Onward, Upward

A Lifelong Journey toward Anti-Oppression and Inclusion in Museums

Cecile Shellman

ROWMAN & LITTLEFIELD
Lanham • Boulder • New York • London

Published by Rowman & Littlefield
An imprint of The Rowman & Littlefield Publishing Group, Inc.
4501 Forbes Boulevard, Suite 200, Lanham, Maryland 20706
www.rowman.com

86-90 Paul Street, London EC2A 4NE

British Library Cataloguing in Publication Information Available

Library of Congress Cataloging-in-Publication Data

Names: Shellman, Cecile, author.
Title: Inward, outward, onward, upward : a lifelong journey towards
  anti-oppression and inclusion in museums / Cecile Shellman.
Other titles: Lifelong journey towards anti-oppression and inclusion in
  museums
Description: Lanham : Rowman & Littlefield, [2024] | Publication supported
  by the American Alliance of Museums. | Includes bibliographical
  references and index. | Summary: "Inward, Outward, Onward, Upward is
  about the personal connection each individual must have to the work of
  anti-oppression and inclusion. Prompts, dialogue-starters, illustrations
  and charts are among the exercises that gently guide, encourage
  alignment, and begin to unearth the puzzling impediments to real
  growth"— Provided by publisher.
Identifiers: LCCN 2024014741 (print) | LCCN 2024014742 (ebook) | ISBN
  9781538193068 (cloth) | ISBN 9781538193075 (paperback) | ISBN
  9781538193082 (ebook)
Subjects: LCSH: Museums and minorities—United States. | Museums—United
  States—Management. | Organizational change—United States. |
  Anti-racism—United States. | Social integration—United States.
Classification: LCC AM11 .S55 2024 (print) | LCC AM11 (ebook) | DDC
  069/.108—dc23/eng/20240402

LC record available at https://lccn.loc.gov/2024014741
LC ebook record available at https://lccn.loc.gov/2024014742

♾™ The paper used in this publication meets the minimum requirements of American
National Standard for Information Sciences—Permanence of Paper for Printed Library
Materials, ANSI/NISO Z39.48-1992.

I dedicate this book to all the museum clients and friends I
have met and worked with, striven and laughed with, cried and
prayed with, even though I am not a praying woman.

The work is not easy.

Committing to change your museum means committing to change yourself,
and this can be difficult. I, too, was in your shoes many years ago, and
I hope that my words can assure you that there is hope and strength in
shared struggle. There's love in learning, power in each one of us.

The work is only beginning.

Be patient but be diligent. I hope this book helps.

Acknowledgments

Thank you to my husband, Dr. Spencer Shellman, who loved and encouraged me through a spectacularly difficult year and whose love has been undeniable throughout the past twenty.

To Charles Harmon, editor at Rowman & Littlefield, who sat with us at a small table over coffee in New York City. I knew I wanted to work with you again the minute we met in person.

To Sam, whose gestural cartoons essentialize each lesson they're meant to teach.

To all the friends and colleagues whose kindness and hope have helped me heal in 2023: Cristee Campbell; Solange and Sandra, manas do meu coraçao; Judy O'Toole; Priya, my lovely neighbor; Linda Budd; Leah Morelli; Edith Doron; Marla Nortman; Grace Stewart; and Dr. Johnnetta Betsch Cole. Thank you.

Contents

Preface

Nine years ago, I sat in my small, cramped office on the first floor of a prestigious museum, timidly pressing buttons on the phone to cold-call other museums about their diversity and inclusion strategies. Surely, other museums had a chief officer responsible for leading, training, monitoring, and directing their efforts to eradicate bias, hire representationally, and advise curators on best practices.

"Yes, I'll hold." I would be holding for a long time in some cases. Most museums back then had not considered such practices. Fortuitously, over time I happened upon one or two others in the field who like me, had recently been enjoined by their museums to improve company culture, train staff in intercultural approaches, and diversify staff and board as to race and ethnicity. We enjoyed periodic phone calls even as we remarked about being pioneers in this realm. We met at conferences and encouraged changemakers to encourage such positions in their museums too. We found the ear of museum association leaders who seated us on committees and entreated us to assist practitioners system-wide to advocate for this model as needed.

Those were joyful and creative times. I was grateful to be numbered among their ranks, to learn with and from them, to apply principles of anti-oppression and inclusion in my own life and community, and to make lifelong friends in far-flung places.

In the ensuing years, there's hardly been a museum that does not have some kind of strategy, planned or ongoing, to address their justice concerns. I have counseled scores of them as a successful consultant. I've worked with their teams, their board members, and their executive directors to coach them on basics and to ensure that their internal culture will sustain the changes they're initiating. I have spoken at conferences and convenings, university podiums, and my kitchen table via a humble laptop at online events. My colleagues and comrades have too. Admirably, professional museum organizations and academia have applied foci to DEAI as an essential tenet of museology.

But nearly ten years on, it's clear there's no happily ever after. Despite numerous published articles and tomes, workshops and trainings, trials and errors, many museums remain stymied about the purpose of their DEAI work, who's responsible for it, and what it should entail.

I've long been enamored with the salutation "Onward and upward!" It seems a genial, positive nod to a traveler on a common road, acknowledging our shared path and encouraging the other to keep moving and to keep their eyes forward. I would apply this valediction sometimes in speech and writing to despondent clients who were doing what needed to be done and who were not seeing immediate results.

One day, in preparation for an online workshop with a favorite museum client, I felt a wave of inspiration. I could see why some of the DEAI efforts weren't bearing fruit. It was clear that many of the wonderful, faithful, dear museum professionals with whom I was working were struggling to internalize the messages I was teaching. They wanted to have an answer soon and a solution now. They wanted me to tell their leaders what to do and for the whole staff to bear witness. There were few museums of which I was aware that had healthy internal communication, and I realized that working together, with each staff member and leader committing to the same degree at the same time, was the only way these initiatives could be fully successful. It was difficult: The same oppressive qualities we were trying to condemn ran rife in the museum halls and offices, too, despite the staff's insistence that it just wasn't so. Unless there is integrity and unless each individual takes accountability and works together in the institution, change will not soon happen.

My 2022 book, *Effective Diversity, Equity, Accessibility, Inclusion, and Anti-Racism Practices for Museums*, discusses this notion somewhat, but the clarion call is not clear.

This book, *Inward, Outward, Onward, Upward: A Lifelong Journey toward Anti-Oppression and Inclusion in Museums*, is a more incisive look at diversity, equity, accessibility, inclusion, anti-racism, pro-marginalized people, and museums. It asks its readers—museum professionals, paraprofessionals, museum governing bodies, and museum academic programs—to practice the skills of looking inward, developing empathy, working collaboratively across the museum to address the systemic effects of unexamined oppression, and working tirelessly for justice and change.

DEAI—or whatever permutation of initials one might apply to this complex, critical concern—is not just about who leads museums and what they look like. It's about acknowledging and redressing harms to people who have been, and continue to be, unjustly neglected, unfairly treated, willfully minoritized, and historically hidden from museums. It's about looking at both the people and the systems that have caused harm and seeking to ameliorate them. It's about being generous enough, brave enough, and vulnerable enough to learn from other people about ourselves, our shared motivations, beliefs, and practices, and to heal our world from the inside out.

In 2023, while recuperating from a major illness, I designed an interactive professional development game for museum teams called THE WORK. Sequential card prompts and games help practitioners think about their relationships to self and community as they create dialogue together. A few months later, I met with my Rowman & Littlefield editor, realizing I had at least another book in me. It's been a quick but glorious few months, and I'm grateful for the opportunity to tell more of the story and offer more tools to help us talk, think, and work together.

Part I
Inward

1

Start with Yourself

A JOURNEY WITHIN

The summer of 2020 is one that will forever be marked as a pivot point and touchstone. A season of chaos and confusion, sadness and loss, fear and frustration, and rage and helplessness descended on us suddenly and incrementally as we were forced to reckon with our shared humanity in an environment of impending oblivion.

On a terrible night in late May 2020, I sat transfixed for hours in my small Pittsburgh living room viewing video clip after video clip of a forty-six-year-old Black man's last minutes on this planet, his final breaths snuffed out by a smirking policeman bearing his knee on the victim's neck with alarming savagery. I watched helplessly online as the mourning in his native Minneapolis spilled out into the streets and tears spilled down the faces of so many anguished people, fists raised, voices raging, and angst blazing a collective force and energy that was electric and unstoppable. With orders to stay in due to the coronavirus pandemic that summer, I was not well enough to protest, but I did in spirit, following along on live streams of my friends' own organized marches from doorstep to city steps and streets, to churches, to community and city centers, all over the country and in different countries too.

So much passion, so much pain.

Just six or seven months prior in my city of Pittsburgh, my neighborhood of Squirrel Hill had endured a different, but related, unimaginable loss—a hateful malcontent had entered a synagogue and laid waste to members of a Jewish community in prayer.

Outside, the rage, the tumult, the hubris of it all swirled in actuality and in my growing imagination as I consumed ever more information about the various happenings and goings-on.

Many tears were shed in my household over the inhumanity and brutality of human to human.

Internally, I was also at unrest.

The COVID-19 remain-in-place orders of the previous few months were bad enough. They made hermits out of my husband and me. Ordinarily, we were get-up-and-go kind of folks, always hither and yon in a tizzy of work trips or quick, distant vacations. Coronavirus forced us to hunker down, to make ourselves smaller and more present with each other and with life in general. It forced us to be more vulnerable, more open, more truthful. Crisis had wrought this.

I found myself continually asking two questions that summer to myself and to my loved ones: "How did this happen?" and "What can I do?" These questions were equally referencing the murder of George Floyd, the global pandemic, and the killing of people at prayer in their neighborhood synagogue a year and a half before.

I fought the impulse of questioning myself and my power to do anything against the bitterness of the world. After all, it was their fault. Whoever they were, and whatever their barbarous malfeasance, Someone Else had done this and Someone Else needed to exact justice to make everything right. My job was to be chagrined, outraged, upset, and vocal. Ultimately, nothing would get done, and the world would return to a state of unrest of another kind later, but such was the way of things. Who was I to question it?

The more I considered this, the less true it rang. My passion, my intellect, my soul, and my commitment did, indeed, have a place in this fight for a better world.

The fight against racism, xenophobia, disinformation, and violence requires each of us as individuals, community members, and citizens of nations and of the world to enter with bravery and compassion and vanquish the forces that seek harm.

Quite suddenly, it seemed, in mid-2020 corporations and nonprofit organizations began organically publishing statements of acknowledgment, support, and contrition in solidarity with the grieving families of the prematurely dead, against the naked racism and brutal hatred that seemed to have gone unchecked allowing these monstrous happenings to occur. Citing the brutal police aggression, museums and other groups forcefully decried organizational and systemic racism. With fervent hope, they penned earnest, heartwarming missives claiming to sympathize and to show their support.

I was especially bemused when a museum with which I'm deeply familiar published a statement extolling its anti-racist values. Merely three years prior, its director had told me that not only was anti-racism not a focus of the museum—what should be next, Save the Whales? After all, museums were not supposed to be champions of social causes.

It was sometimes hard to separate the statement from the source's integrity.

When museum leaders began asking for my help in crafting solidarity statements against racism, I turned the question inward. Instead of creating a formula for every museum to use, I started asking—what do you truly believe about what happened on the afternoon of May 25, 2020? Even more importantly, what do you believe about racism, anti- LGBTQIA+ sentiment, anti-Semitism, hate crimes, racial violence, sexism, gender bias, and other forms of oppression in society and nationwide? If you have opinions about these issues, and if you truly decry the violence that took the life of George Floyd, be transparent in your statement about the pandemic of hatred and violence that still infects the nation. Your statement will assure the public that you believe you have the power to do something about it as a museum and as stewards of your organization.

While no two thinking adults will believe exactly the same thing and word their thoughts in the same way, an organization whose members face the same direction and use their energies for good will avail much in service of their goals. This kind of organization is perceived as strong and cohesive. Working together to use their common facilities and faculties for good is commendable and inspirational. Leaders have power by virtue of their placement in the organization, the confidence bestowed on them, and their onerous tasks. Those with the power to be changemakers have the responsibility to make healthy, life-affirming changes for the good of all people. The summer of 2020 was a moment to not simply send condolences but also to publicly make strong acknowledgments about the nature of powerful institutions that had long benefited from privilege, followed by real work to redress disparities, inequities, and injustice.

Start there.

Whether writing a single statement or developing an entire approach for a museum's DEAI initiative, every leader, staff member, volunteer, and visitor must begin by looking in the mirror.

In the same way I realized that the clamor outside needed to be quelled by action, care, devotion, and love, so, too, would the turmoil within. These are parallel forces and can be dual realities working together.

If a museum claims to be an anti-oppressive space and treats its employees disdainfully and inappropriately, where is the truth in that? If its leadership team members are bigoted or out of touch, those attributes will deleteriously affect their relationships with internal and external constituents.

I recall a conversation from several years ago when I was speaking with a former museum leader to whom I reported. We were discussing the nature of ongoing DEAI training that I was developing with the support of outside consultants and an internal DEAI working group team. I raised the idea that it was essential for museum leaders to be circumspect, exemplary in moral rectitude, and impartial in their relationships with others. I was challenged to think otherwise, to consider that it wasn't anyone else's business how leaders behaved or what they believed in private and that they had the right to act however they wanted. Additionally, I was told, museums need to be pro causes, not anti. Anti-racism was not a value that should be upheld. I was stunned.

Integrity is a key value in the work of Diversity, Equity, Accessibility, and Inclusion. Integrity simply means wholeness. As it is on the outside, it must be on the inside. If the right side is round, the left must mirror its curvilinear shape. If the expectation is enhanced learning, appreciation, and practice on the outside, this parallelism must happen on an internal and inner-community basis as well. Answering the big questions and confronting turmoil outside our windows demand looking internally through our windows into our own hearths and hearts to tend to the dissent and misunderstanding there as well.

Everyone in your organization must take part, at the same time, and with the same intensity for your initiative to be part of your museum's cultural practice. Only then can it take root as a norm and contribute to the change you seek.

It cannot be handled like a program. It's not a performance.

It cannot be handled as a road map, especially when you don't know where you are going.

It's not a sell. It's not transactional.

It is a new ethic. It is a part of you.

MY OWN JOURNEY TO LOOK INWARD

Some of my favorite life memories have been in art spaces, primarily museums. I started my career in a beautifully appointed three-story gallery in Park City in the early 1990s. It was here I learned to contextualize art, promote artists, use an electronic stud detector, and host art receptions. My clients ranged from television and movie stars like Tom Berenger and Chris Noth to local Utahns buying original paintings on a layaway plan. One of my first assignments was to curate and host a showcase of new artists' work. The exhibition was an enormous success, with nearly every painting and sculpture sold, but most importantly the young artists were launched and poised for success in a blossoming market when the Sundance Film Festival was beginning to come into its own.

From there, I transitioned to working in a church museum where I learned how to manage a large and thriving museum store, eventually became a curator, and wrote training materials for incoming volunteer docents. Along with these skills, I quickly learned not to wear black clothing, which some associated with the devil himself. I was required to wear pantyhose and skirts and modest shoes instead of my slinky unitards with stilettos and tomato-red pantsuits, to which I'd become accustomed. I learned to be more deferential and submissive than I was inclined to be. I bristled at some of the rules. There was so much love here though: There were opportunities for staff and volunteers to truly get to know each other. We worked together, prayed and sang together, exchanged white elephant gifts, and engaged in myriad customs unique to the dominant culture. It didn't seem to matter much that I was the only Black employee, even though there were also many questions and challenges I faced in that environment that bestowed me an advanced degree in code-switching and remaining mum.

My move to the eastern part of the United States a few years later brought intense culture shock. I was immersed in museology—a subject I adored—and had quickly befriended some incredible people. My volunteer stints and work at local museums were the familiar glue that held me together, even as I navigated homesickness, a faith transition, and the aftermath of 9/11. I met and married my husband in the Boston area, at a museum, of course, and through it all was supported by affirming museum experiences and colleagues.

In the ensuing years as my life and work responsibilities gained color and texture in new towns and different surroundings, the luster of museum-as-magical-milieu dimmed, even as the allure lingered. The wonder of these cabinets of curiosity, these infotainment temples, these jewel boxes that were palaces to the people was tempered by the personalities and practices that were mired in trenchant systems.

There were still magical moments, many of them. There were also deeply disturbing challenges at the personal and systemic levels that I couldn't quite shake. There was nowhere to raise concerns, and it constantly felt like nothing would ever, ever change.

At one job in the early 2000s, I was offered a starting salary of twenty thousand dollars—not two hundred thousand, but twenty, which I took anyway because the market was just that competitive, or so they told me. Executive directors in the cultural arts realm were comfortably earning in the six-figure range while their direct reports earned relative pennies on their dollar. As I grew in my career and practice, I saw through the gleaming vitrines and bejeweled hands shaking (handshaking) to the unhappy demeanors of dissatisfied employees, perpetually angry or overstressed bosses, and too little compensation.

There was also a deeply ugly throughline of racial discrimination and disparity in some of these places of employment. It was almost as if museums were an unspoken bastion of privilege and separation. Systemically, it was expressed in the intentional lack of new hires or promotions of color. It was expressed in one-on-one bullying and name-calling, even by those in higher positions. There were few, if any, people of color on the boards of directors and other governing teams. Inappropriate so-called jokes about other minorities were tolerated and indulged. Exhibits minimizing and tokenizing non-European art and culture abounded. This may have happened—surely must have happened—in other museums I'd previously experienced, but I was only starting to notice it, especially as it more pointedly began to affect me and my work.

To their credit, a few of the organizations I worked with championed new programs aiming to ameliorate racial and ethnic disparities in access, funding, provision, and employment. I was hired to supervise or direct more than one of these programs, but the Revolving Door of the Woman of Color operated in my case just as it did for my successors, as even those programs were a function of patriarchy, white supremacy culture, and continued colonialism. A well-meaning foundation would seed a short-term program with lofty multicultural aims in dire circumstances. There was no support and no road map and a preponderance of scrutinous skepticism. Even though the teachers, students, and teaching artists seemed to benefit from the program, it was prematurely concluded. Standards applied ex post facto were not met.

Furthermore, the programs' success measures were deemed more valuable than the actual successes: Goodharting at its best. Goodhart's Law, as stated by statistician Goodhart, is that "When a measure becomes a target, it ceases to become a good measure." In an oppressive system that values the comfort of its leaders' privilege over the well-being of the team and the individuals who comprise it, there is ample room for disingenuously overvaluing the rubric to disenfranchise the person actually doing the work.

I struggled to temper increasingly bitter feelings as I tried with little success to effect lasting change in DEAI in the museum. There was the omnipresent undercurrent imposter syndrome as I realized that my jobs were not only one of a kind, created for me, but I was also one of the very few people of color in a responsible managerial role. This meant that I was closely monitored and scrutinized and my creative, sometimes brilliant, ways of problem-solving were too harshly and prematurely judged, sometimes as cultural misfits or "not the way we usually do things around here." As for the community outreach and program planning aspects of my work, it was easy to organize the one-off programs or program a day of cultural performances showcasing exotic others' "homegrown" talents. I cringed inwardly sometimes and wondered whether (I was) perpetuating narratives that further exoticized nonwhite and immigrant communities but justified it by the compensation being offered to the artists. Supporting them financially was critical. It was weirdly satisfying at the time to believe this was best practice in the visual and performing arts field and was rarely questioned. The default answer to being inclusive was celebrating one's ancestral home country heritage.

The more I found fault, the more uneasy I felt. It was easy to blame the system and the leaders for habits and policies that aggrandized some people and cultures and minimized others. It was as if museums were intended to be exclusive rather than inclusive. Museums were for the hoi polloi, but just like that name for the masses, they were out of touch and impressed by their artful exclusivity.

LOOK INSIDE

I wasn't the only one who noticed. As one of the few arts practitioners; workers; or later, administrators of color who worked in my museums, I had the ear of colleagues and some leaders, many of whom wanted to know my cultural perspective on circumstances in the museum or simply wished to vent. The upsetting things I'd personally experienced or noticed sometimes paled in comparison to what I heard from others. It was chilling and deeply disturbing. But I was a mid-level employee at the time, even when in terms of title, I had ascended to the highest organizational level in the museum. There was no one else within the museum to whom a report could be made. Many of us feared our stories would not be believed or would be minimized. Some employees feared retribution, having a vague sense that speaking ill of the way the museum was run would result in swift and terrible punishment.

In huddled clusters or behind the closed doors of my capacious book-lined office, I gave my earnest advice, but my position, title notwithstanding, did not bestow upon me the necessary power to ameliorate their situations. I increased my ability to listen empathetically and compassionately. My few attempts to call for individual or systemic solutions did not fare well, so I stopped asking for them.

The Plan was the Thing for which I was hired. The Plan. Where is The Plan? Despite having several revisions of a beautifully written DEAI plan at the ready, it was difficult to activate it.

Some museum staff members and leadership wanted an empirical road map to follow that would stack against other museums' plans despite the fact that it was one of the only museums worldwide to have a dedicated DEAI senior officer in place: me.

Others blamed the senior staff and board of directors for any and all equity and inclusion failures at the museum, whether interpersonal, cultural, or system-wide. They wanted a plan that emanated from and was ratified by the organizational power brokers.

Still others expected to be exempt from any work besides critique. They wanted to be the finger-pointers and blame The Leaders (including myself at this point) for not working hard enough.

I decided to stem my feelings of helplessness by practicing what I was starting to preach.

First, Journey inward. Take care of the Inside.

Embarking on a DEAI endeavor at a museum is not for the faint of heart. Museums are typically open to the public more than 300 days a year, with many employees and volunteers working tirelessly under impossible time frames. Asking them to do one more thing seems onerous, but it is essential. At the same time, this ask is the most critical request and commitment that can be made if an institution-wide initiative is to be successful.

Each and every museum member must commit to doing the work, even before a formal plan is initiated. They must commit to being open; listening to others; collaborating in new ways; and most importantly, being willing to be altruistic for the sake of a more just museum and world. Everyone should bring their best selves and honest efforts to the challenge at whatever level they are and with whatever learning they currently possess.

If the DEAI goal of the museum is to materially change the museum's outlook and significantly address social issues at the systemic level, each museum worker should be able to determine whether this is a set of values they agree to uphold and a direction they are comfortable taking. It is not the leaders' job alone to figure out the challenges and make the changes. After all, patriarchy and colonialism are among the principles to be investigated and dismantled. If that's the case, each and every person belonging to the museum must contribute and have a voice and use it.

Know that you can effect change and that you have the power to understand, contribute, communicate, and be successful.

It requires empathy and understanding to do this work. Leaders are not necessarily taught these skills on their road to the top, and some humans will unknowingly repeat old patterns that encourage the ill-treatment of subordinates because that's the cultural norm.

Junior employees learn to fear their managers and directors; it's almost an expectation that their bosses will be distant at best and viciously mean at worst. How many of us, despite ourselves, cackle cathartically at the wild antics of characters in revenge fantasy movies or Victorian novels? If we must punch, punch up.

The work of DEAI is people centered, justice focused, and collaborative. If we don't have empathy and compassion and we can't see ourselves in each other, no list of to-dos will help us become more inclusive and cohesive.

A high-level museum employee once approached me, complaining, "All I want to do is look at the pretty paintings on the wall." It may very well be that you, too, see this as your focus when your museum may outpace you in an overarching, more noble ethic of protecting marginalized communities and seeking justice. Analyzing and acknowledging one's own commitment level is, therefore, the first step. A last step for some after refusing to participate might be leaving the institution in search of a better fit.

If a museum leader is working on a plan in isolation with little collaboration or input and without the collegiality and support of fellow staff and leaders, the initiative will die on the vine.

If there's enough desire to change and you do things right no matter how arduous and lengthy the process, it can be done.

A biblical story tells of a man beleaguered with sores covering his body. He asks what he should do to be healed, and God tells him to wash in a common river seven times. The remedy described seems so simple, and even fatuous.

At first, Naaman refuses to do such a silly thing. As he continues to resist, the disease worsens, and his distress is prolonged. When he finally acquiesces, at the nadir of his suffering, his complexion changes to the smooth, dewy texture of a child's.

We have to embody our beginnings. We are our own best healers. Trust the remedy, simple though it may seem. Trust yourselves, your colleagues, and your museum to try something new to resolve painful and perplexing issues.

The process toward self-actualization involves the following:

- Self (looking inward)
- Others around us (conversing and looking outward, learning to work harmoniously with others in service of the same goal)
- The larger community (onward)
- The more expanded systems (upward)

Museums are at varying stages of creating and diving into DEAI plans. In the last two or three years, I have seen and commented on scores of plans—everything from single-page lists to dense numbered theses. There's really no right or wrong way to initiate a plan. It must be in your museum's own voice, its own culture, and relate to all other strategies connected to the major activities of the organization. It must have a sense of seriousness and importance that is felt at every level of the organization and must suit the culture of the company seamlessly.

Wherever you are, start now to involve your full selves, your ability to dialogue with colleagues, your sworn values and commitments, and your work in your community. Don't abandon any of your current work but understand your work should go deeper at a more significant level than you may at first recognize. It will also take longer than you realize, and that's OK.

Note well: The plan is not the list of activities. The plan is the strategy by which the museum will accomplish the goal.

WHAT IS THE GOAL?

The goal cannot simply be to comply with best practices, copy another entity's award-winning strategy, or win a grant award. The plan cannot prioritize hiring people from nonwhite ethnicities without analyzing the museum, your community, and your constituents to gauge whether you can truly welcome, support, and assist them in decolonizing your museum. After all, the long-term goal should be one of justice. It should be seeking to provide succor and hope to those who have been emotionally, physically, and psychologically harmed by organizations like yours. The strategy to achieve such is unique to each museum. The organization must bravely and with vulnerability uncover what is unjust about the museum, its relationship to the larger community, and its treatment of all who support it and then commit to ameliorating the unjust conditions.

Agreeing to accept the imperative of a DEAI and justice-forward ethic means that an organization must realize that its raison d'être has forever changed. No longer is a zoological garden just a zoo, a science museum just a museum, or an aquarium simply an aquarium. The organization has taken on the mantle of championing equity through its programs, practices, personnel, and its very presence.

Without this overarching goal, a DEAI plan is a list of activities that is temporary and strategic. It risks being lackluster, performative, and expensive. Not only could it be costly monetarily, it could cost relationships across communities seeking help and hope from institutions claiming to be public facing. It could cause tension among the leadership, staff, visitors, funders, and directors of the museum who may have wildly differing opinions about how involved museums should be in its justice-seeking efforts.

TRANSPARENCY

Next, communicate this overarching goal to everyone across the museum. Your museum may not currently be the kind of place that feels like home or is like a family. However, in today's world, which is filled with trauma, continued violence, pain, and division, the museum must come together, hunker down, and engage in tough love to build trust and forge an environment of psychological safety: Things must change.

I have known museum boards and directors whose staff had no idea that their museum had committed to a DEAI strategy years prior. In other museums, a group of passionate staff members organically convenes to make changes in and throughout the museum, but they lack the power to communicate their intentions system-wide.

Garnering feedback from all of the stakeholders of the museum and then inviting a predetermined number to serve as a working group to shape the initiative is one way to start with transparency and purpose. The working group can be the liaison between the leadership and the other staff and volunteers.

A WORD ABOUT WORKING GROUPS

Museums come in all shapes and sizes, but, nonetheless, there are some practices that garner best results when entered into collaboratively, valuing input from varied voices. Like a choir's, the internalized message of a museum can be resonant and impactful when fortified by voices of different tones, strengths, abilities, and vantage points. That said, some museums will have massive, overwhelming voices—massive choirs whose voices dominate merely by virtue of size. Other museums may only have a sweet trio or duet. Their effectiveness might surprise you. Their use of dynamics, the ingenuity of a unique musical arrangement, or the dulcet tones that take your breath away might be even more relevant for the moment than a larger group with more brio. Your museum may have only a soloist despite the desire for a sizable working group, committee, department, or division. As with all aspects of the counsel I provide, think about the nature of your own circumstance and adjust accordingly. Do you have a robust choir that is eager but has not been trained in basic music theory? If so, you have work to do. Your choir, duet, or whatever it may currently be represents those who can currently be the thought and action leaders for your institution's DEAI initiative.

But what if there is no megaphone or microphone to amplify the small voice or two no matter how sweet? If the voice can't be heard or it will be disparaged and disregarded, the group of two must access additional power from someone with authority to do so and with the promise of advocacy and continual support.

Whatever the size of your working group, explain to your leadership, board, and staff that the work requires commitment from each person. If possible, hold a meeting and ask those who agree to show agreement to be open to DEAI efforts in some observable way. This is the new direction of the museum and will be an expectation going forward.

A good DEAI initiative will include weaving values of representation and anti-oppression throughout the practices and procedures of the museum—both formal and informal ones. Convey to your staff and others that among the expectations may be the following:

- Regular and frequent participation
- Staff workshops and training, including the following:

  - Onboarding and HR employee expectations.
  - Department-specific training about how colonialism, bias, prejudice, and privilege functioned historically and continue to persist systemically in each discipline area of a museum and of other large institutions that are slow to integrate and operate healthily across cultures.
  - Team-building activities that teach as they entertain. Team-building topics should include cultural proficiency, handling microaggressions, understanding the museum job environment, and crisis managment.
  - Supervisory and management training that focuses on people skills, effective project management, and conflict resolution.

- New models of meeting, planning, and working together that prioritize collaboration, taking time to interact with relevant parties to gain necessary feedback so they are valued, and treating all contributors with the dignity and respect they deserve.
- Eager participation in activities and improved work culture.
- Additional creative work to investigate and develop interventions, skills, and techniques to decanter dominant narratives, democratize certain processes, work more closely with marginalized communities, and implement overall behaviors that demonstrate a shared commitment to justice and equity.

The management team and DEAI working group should formalize their early evolving thoughts about DEAI work at the museum by writing brief documents giving shape to the initiative based on existing museum materials; best practices for the field; and input from staff, leadership, and board members, including the following:

- Statement of purpose
- Communications blurb
- List of activities
- Shared definitions
- Brief list of readings, podcasts, documentaries, related fiction, and so on

Copies of these materials should be printed and distributed to every stakeholder and included as addenda in policy manuals, bylaws, strategic planning documents, and other internal material.

After a museum shares its desire for a thoroughgoing DEAI focus with the staff in person and via email and printed letters, it can set the expectation for all stakeholders to do some private but collective soul-searching.

I suggest a few exercises to help you get started on your Inward journey:

1. Journaling
2. Who I Am
3. I Am, But I Am not
4. Examining My Bias
5. I Feel, I Think, I Believe
6. Museums and Me

No matter the size, type, or nature of your museum, everyone can and should participate in these activities.

1. JOURNALING

The DEAI working group team and museum management should announce in as many forms possible that (a) their DEAI initiative is about to take shape and (b) that it will require a long-standing commitment from each constituent. The announcement should include some language about the intent to collaborate with staff and welcome ideas from them. One element of this commitment is for each person to decide and document how they truly feel about issues pertaining to anti-oppression and inclusion.

Writing is an excellent way to begin a DEAI journey. Encourage the activity of writing as much as possible. Distribute identical high-quality aesthetically attractive journals to the staff, perhaps including a nice writing implement or bookmark, as a gift to mark this momentous occasion.

No one should be exempt from this exercise—not board members, volunteers, staff members, interns, managers, leadership teams, or ancillary staff. This is one of the activities that everyone can truly say they participated in together.

The Inward activities, particularly the journal writing, should be confidential and private. Employees should not be made to share their writings with anyone, especially not with those who have supervisory authority. This exercise should be a fun and freeing one.

Journaling may comprise single sentences of text or effusive paragraphs or pages in a single writing session. Participants should be given latitude and choice, especially where some of them may not experience freedom to choose much else in their work lives. Because the entire subject pertains to respecting culture and individuality, the journal writing alone is an affirming practice that demonstrates the organization's concern for the emotional growth of the whole person in their care.

A journal writer may decide to write about only specific museum matters, or perhaps they might make connections to other aspects of their life that touch on unity, justice, anti-oppression, and bridge building. They may find that sermons from their faith community, meditations in their yoga practice, strategies in their chess game, or lyrics to their best beats have relevance to the museum's stated goals of inclusion and justice.

Journal writers may unearth a panoply of emotions and truths about themselves and their relationships with others that they might not be prepared to reveal to others. That's OK. It's important for those connected with museums to know they have the freedom to think and express a wide range of positive and negative opinions about the way the institution is run, what it collects, who it serves, and what the future portends. At a later time, they may be able to express these opinions to the right people at the right time to advance strategic goals of the institution. Before that, and in a private venue, they should be able to clearly express what they mean to say.

HOW THE MUSEUM CAN HELP TO SHAPE THE JOURNALING EFFORTS

For the journaling exercise, to prime the pump the DEAI working group could decide on one question per week to be posed group-wide.

Here are 101 such questions for inspiration. You may wish to come up with your own questions—perhaps even more pointed questions relevant to your particular museum and community.

1. What do you enjoy most about working here?
2. What irks you most about the museum as a worker, stakeholder, or visitor?
3. Do you think the museum values its employees? What informs your opinion?

4. What commitment can you bring to ensure a more diverse museum environment and community over time?
5. Do you feel emotionally, psychologically, and physically safe at this museum?
6. Describe one equitable practice you wish the museum would undertake immediately for the benefit of the staff.
7. Think about your unique identities, background, culture, and community. Are you among the minority or majority at the museum? How does that affect the way you behave or the way you are treated?
8. Remember your first day on the job as compared to today. How did you feel then versus now? What changed?
9. Name three habits you would like to change at the museum to build relationships and be more collegial at the museum.
10. Write a private letter to your supervisor and either thank or complain to them regarding the way they treat you and your colleagues.
11. Do you feel valued at the museum? By whom, and how can you tell?
12. Do you feel invisible or unwanted at the museum? When is it most evident, and why do you feel this way?
13. What is your favorite exhibit at the museum?
14. If you have or someone you know has a disability, how easy might it be for them to navigate the physical or mental spaces at the museum?
15. What's your favorite museum object and why?
16. What attracted you to the museum field?
17. If you've ever had professional development about museum practice, and particularly around DEAI; justice in museum spaces; and anti-oppression, write about your experience. If not, research an upcoming opportunity and write a draft of a letter asking your supervisor to send you.
18. Write a poem or short essay about gender bias, racial discrimination, LGBTQIA+ exclusion, or similar harms at your museum.
19. Why did you choose to work for the museum?
20. Should museums be neutral on social issues, or should they collectively express opinions and endorse a position?
21. Remember the last museum exhibition you viewed at this or any other museum that challenged dominant narratives and centered another perspective. What do you think about the exhibition's message and content?
22. Who is your favorite artist, scientist, historian, or author who is from a different ethnic or racial background than your own?
23. How could one of the projects you are working on currently be improved to provide a more inclusive and accessible environment? Who on your team could make this happen?
24. Write a review of your museum as if you were visiting it for the first time. Hold nothing back! Give praise where warranted.

25. Who is your best friend or ally at the museum? Do you have someone in whom you can confide?
26. What is your earliest memory of meeting someone from a different age group, ethnic group, country, or religion that the group you are or were from?
27. What is the makeup of your work team or your museum colleagues? How diverse or homogeneous is it in terms of age, gender, race, nationality, sexual orientation, economic background, and educational background as far as you know?
28. What do you know about the founding of your museum?
29. What kind of philanthropic activities is your museum known for if any? What would you like to see the museum do in that arena?
30. When was the last time you had a conversation with someone outside of your work group at the museum? What was it about?
31. Do you feel comfortable speaking with those with greater or lesser responsibility and authority at the museum? Why or why not?
32. When was the last time you sat and listened to someone outside of your racial or ethnic group speak assertively on a museum-related topic for more than an hour?
33. Are there currently exclusive cliques, factions, or groups—unofficial or sanctioned—that exist at the museum? What does it take to become a participating member and how does this make you feel?
34. Can you remember a time when you intervened to help someone who was being treated poorly or who was marginalized at the museum? Write about it, or if you have not done this, what do you think you would do?
35. From a scale of 1 to 10, with one being mildly important to 10 being essential, where does DEAI fall for you? Give a number and jot down why.
36. What's your favorite museum to visit?
37. Where would you be working if not at this museum?
38. What is your favorite article about inclusion?
39. What's your favorite book about anti-racism?
40. Whom do you admire most in life?
41. What has working at the museum taught you about empathy and compassion?
42. Considering your job duties and daily activities, what kind of power do you have at the museum?
43. Which group, organization, or community is doing admirable work in service of museum equity and inclusion? How did you come to know about them?
44. When was the last time you had a conversation with a museum colleague about diversity, equity, accessibility, and inclusion at the museum?
45. What is your favorite quote about social justice?
46. What are your hopes for the museum's DEAI strategy?

47. If you have worked somewhere else that had a successful DEAI practice, what were the most effective aspects of their program?
48. Explain a museum to someone from outer space. What does a museum do, whom does it serve, why, for what purpose, et cetera.
49. What was the most fun you had at the museum or at a museum function away from your current museum?
50. What was your unhappiest day at the museum?
51. Is your inclination more to work in solitude or to collaborate with others?
52. Do you enjoy meeting, talking to, and working with people from other cultures and backgrounds?
53. Read a news article about a current social justice issue. In what ways does this issue pertain to you, and to what degree?
54. Read an article about current museum challenges in implementing anti-oppression strategies. Do you notice commonalities and differences between these and your own museum's?
55. Do you feel respected and heard at your museum? Why or why not?
56. Do you feel comfortable talking about your feelings and opinions with your colleagues?
57. Do you believe you have the ability to make changes at the museum? In what ways?
58. Define for yourself the terms diversity, equity, accessibility, inclusion, justice, and belonging
59. Define appropriation and appreciation.
60. Have there been any significant events in your life that allowed you to think more expansively about your worldview, changing the way you see life and react to other people?
61. Is there a work of art, exhibition, specimen, research, display, or historical marker that is on display at your museum that is particularly meaningful to you? Have you shared it with others, and what do you say?
62. Do you know whom you could talk to at the museum to get historical information about the staff demographics at the museum over the years, or the diversity of the collections? Are there news articles currently housed in the public libraries or your museum's own library that mention exhibitions created in times past that memorialized important historical events? Research and write about this.
63. When was the last time you performed a random act of kindness for someone at the museum? If never, or if you wish to do another, perform an anonymous act of kindness and discuss it in your journal entry.
64. After entering information in your Who am I exercises below, return to your journal list as many times as possible and continue these activities. First, how easy or difficult is it for you to take a walk down memory lane? Acknowledge that it might not be comfortable.

65. Do you know the difference between race, ethnicity, nationality, culture, and cultural background?
66. Have you ever met people from another race, ethnicity, or nationality who are very much like you culturally? Where are the intersections?
67. What do you know about the difference between the Transatlantic Slave Trade and the Slave Trade in the Americas?
68. What were the major differences between the way enslavement of Africans and people of African descent ended in Brazil, Jamaica, and the United States?
69. What was your most embarrassing moment when discussing or engaging in activities in an intercultural setting? Your answer could involve language barriers, misunderstood cultural behaviors, or comical mistakes.
70. What was your first cross-cultural experience, and what was it like? This could be anything from pen pals to study abroad experiences, vacations, or chance meetings.
71. What grounds you in the deepest moments of unrest, crisis, or and despair?
72. Where do go in the museum to be alone with your thoughts?
73. What work project are you proudest of at this museum?
74. Which community collaborators or organizations have made the most effort in working with our museum?
75. Do you get along with your co-workers? Which ones do you most enjoy?
76. If you frequent the museum's café or restaurant, what are your favorite menu items?
77. If your last or current week at the museum were made into a moving picture or Broadway play, who would play the role of the executive director? Who would play you? What would the most dramatic scene be?
78. Have you considered why Black justice, pro-Blackness, and anti-racism issues are critical to DEAI work?
79. What accessibility features does your museum have or provide for people with disabilities?
80. Do you believe that you should contribute to the museum as a paying member or should employees and other stakeholders be given free membership with all attendant benefits?
81. When was your very first museum visit? What was it like?
82. What latitude or freedom would you like to experience that you do not currently enjoy as a museum practitioner or volunteer at the museum?
83. Would you say a museum is more like an amusement park or more like a university?
84. What are your hopes for museums in the future?
85. What are your fears about museums?
86. What five nonfiction works would you contribute to a reading list for your museum?
87. What are your thoughts about book bans?

88. What are the most egregious barriers that exist to museum access for would-be visitors?
89. What makes a museum successful?
90. How diverse is your museum leadership regarding race, age, ethnicity, nationality, gender, sexual orientation, and other differences that matter in your community?
91. What would you change if you were executive director for a year, and how would you change it? If you are the executive director, substitute board chair..
92. Is music ever played in your museum by individuals, museum staff, pro-grammatically, or continuously in public areas such as the cafeteria? What would you change about those choices?
93. Which museums would you like to visit worldwide, and why?
94. Which museum jobs are the most and the least gender diverse?
95. What is the most profound or impactful lecture you have heard from the podium at your museum?
96. Does your museum leadership have an open-door policy? Who do you feel most comfortable approaching?
97. Do you have friends at other museums with similar job duties? Schedule a conversation with them, ask if you can note it in your private journal, and ask one or two questions from this list as conversation starters.
98. Have you ever noticed bad behavior at the museum and refused to inter-rupt it?
99. Have you ever attended an exhibition opening as a guest at your own museum or another museum? What was it like?
100. If your museum is not diverse as to race, ethnicity, age, socioeconomic status, why is it important to become more diverse?
101. How diverse is diverse enough? How equitable is equitable enough? How inclusive is inclusive enough? How accessible is accessible enough?

Encourage the DEAI team to keep a list of suggested readings, films, and media for staff to read or watch. Having done so, those who are participating in the initiative could write their feelings and thoughts about the evocative material.

During staff meetings and other formal convenings, leaders could remind staff to do their journal work and lead a short discussion about how it's going over time. Leaders may even wish to share how their own practice has strength-ened or changed them in one way or another.

Those who prefer to write daily could do so in addition to setting aside time to respond to the weekly prompts. Daily writings might include musings on an inspirational quote about anti-racism, new awareness about hidden biases or previously unexamined privilege, a critique or commentary on a film that discusses cultural clashes or exchanges; or their own definitions of terms that they encounter regarding diversity, inclusion, and justice-forward work. The exercises over time should encourage authentic expression, contemplation, sharpening observation skills, and speaking about themselves and others in meaningful, productive ways.

2

Worksheets and Exercises to Explore One's Own Beliefs and Capacity

Self-work comprises more than note-taking and musing. The skills that are strengthened through critical thinking, applying compassion, and documenting are only part of the challenge. Ultimately, a thoughtful DEAI project should encourage individuals to practice thinking about, dialoguing with, and alleviating the burdens of others. To do this, one must fully engage in being deeply self-aware and other aware.

The following worksheets and exercises will help to build the metaphorical muscles required to battle for human and civil rights as an individual among others on a team.

WORKSHEETS

WHO AM I?

This worksheet is designed to facilitate self-reflection and understanding of your own heritage, culture, ethnicity, race, socioeconomic status, and other characteristics you may find important. It also may help you to develop compassion for others and use museum exhibits as prompts for comparisons and contrasts or as memory joggers.

1. Have I ever been or am I currently a "black sheep," or outcast, to my family or other beloved formative group for my ideological beliefs?
2. Have I ever shunned anyone because of their beliefs?
3. What aspects of my culture and heritage are most important to me?

Attribute	Notes
My name	
My name origins	
My identity/identities	
My race or ethnicity	
My heritage or background	
My ancestry if known	
My nationality (passport country)	
My family story—How did we arrive where we are geographically?	
My family of origin's religion	
My current religion or spirituality	
My friends and peer group	
My career ambitions	
My education	
My parents' education	
My sibling order and closeness	

4. What do I like most about myself?
5. When was the first time I saw, spoke to, or intentionally befriended specific people who were not like me in terms of age, race, ethnic background, nationality, residence, or spiritual identity?
6. What do I like least about me?

MY IDENTITIES AND MY WORK

1. How does reflecting on my own experiences help me develop compassion toward others at the museum?
2. Have I ever had an interaction with a fellow staff member or a visitor that can be described as compassionate?
3. Do I see my own race, religion, culture, ethnicity, or economic status reflected in the design, content, or production of the museum's exhibits or programs?
4. How do the museum's offerings help me feel and demonstrate compassion toward others?

5. When I look at the museum exhibitions or participate in its programs, do I feel confident in my ability to interpret, derive meaning from, or engage fully with the work?
6. Can I bring my whole self to work and feel comfortable as a representative of the museum and a proud employee of an enterprise I love?

EMBARRASSMENT, SHAME, AND GUILT

Some individuals who are in various stages of thinking about oppression and suffering start to have intense feelings of guilt and shame. These emotions are apt to reveal themselves when discussing similarities and differences across cultures and noticing that there are vast inequities in the lived experiences of others based on their gender, sexual orientation, race, family status, economic status, and other markers.

EMBARRASSMENT

When asked about what they hope to get from a DEAI initiative, many museum workers say they would like to use language that is precise and inclusive when writing, speaking about, or conversing with people from cultures different than their own. In addition to not wanting to offend strangers by mispronouncing names, misgendering them, or betraying a lack of knowledge about their cultures, they say it's because they don't want to embarrass themselves or their institution. No one wants to be canceled, excoriated, misunderstood, or called out for misspeaking. In today's fast-paced digital world, one misstep can seemingly cost a reputation or even a career.

We also want to be well thought of by our colleagues and peers. If someone uses a term to describe a member of a marginalized group, for example, and the term is out of date, a malapropism, or mispronounced, they might be worried they will cause offense and worried about what their peers might think of them for not knowing better. No one knows everything, but today's expectations are that everyone keep up on learning appropriate intercultural language.

SHAME

Another issue facing those who attempt to confront racial bias and oppression is that they claim not to wish to delve into the past due to the feelings of shame that these journeys engender. Whether shame of white ancestors having oppressed, dehumanized, and killed others who were different from them for caprice or financial gain or shame that after centuries some of the systems that allowed these behaviors persist, the emotion is incisive and piquant. After all, these are deeply shameful acts.

Further, some people feel ashamed learning in large-group settings or even working alongside staff members whose cultural and ethnic identities are vastly different from their own, realizing that just a century or two earlier, Black people were not even officially considered human beings by their own government. They feel shame knowing that the United States allowed the transatlantic slave trade; slavery; the separation of families; and rape of men, women, and children to occur. There are movements afoot in the 2020s encouraging the erasure of these historical truths in public libraries and in schools. Museums have a unique opportunity to fill the educational gap created by those who wish to hide the truth in other ways and venues.

GUILT

Guilt is a feeling that happens when we know we have transgressed against a law or norm. The feeling is intensified when we do nothing to repent or make restoration for what we have done. I often hear from clients or lecture attendees that DEAI workshops elicit feelings of guilt in white people and others who experience relative privilege. They complain that it is unfair and not inclusive to pique feelings of guilt in those who do not consciously mean to harm others.

It is important to acknowledge up front that feelings of embarrassment, shame, and guilt will come to many of us during our personal and collective reckoning. It's a hard ask for us to openly dialogue with fellow employees about systems of deep oppression and torture when our own workplaces have been described at times as toxic.

It might be helpful for your museum's human resources department and the DEAI working group to start a lending library or bibliography focused on healing from racial trauma. We don't talk enough about generational trauma and its impact on the workplace or in schools, particularly where it affects the mental and emotional health of people affected by settler colonialism, Native American displacement, the transatlantic slave trade, slavery, the Reconstruction era, Jim Crow, the civil rights movement of the 1950s and 1960s, and Japanese internment, among others.

Feelings of embarrassment, shame, and guilt are complex and natural. Learning to deal with these emotions privately and in public is essential to collaboration on a DEAI initiative. It is through this reckoning—grappling in a raw and vulnerable way with the sins of one's forbears and committing to a justice-forward life are important to the process.

EXERCISE

1. Think of a time when you have felt each emotion—embarrassment, shame, or guilt. Were these feelings justified? How did you come to terms with or resolve these feelings?
2. Think of a time when you observed or perpetrated a microaggression toward someone else. What were the emotions you felt? How did you deal with the situation?

UNDERSTANDING PERSONAL BIAS

We all have biases. It sounds ugly and shameful to say this because most of us want to be thought of as morally upright, rational, and fair. To admit we have biases is to admit a deeper inner working that we neither completely agree with nor understand. Biases gather influences from our personal opinions; lived experiences; and unknown, unconscious stimuli, encouraging us to believe or behave positively or negatively toward a person, group, or thing. We may be so steeped in our biases, thinking that we believe we are making informed decisions from our deeply held viewpoints and lived experiences. Left unchecked, that bias becomes judgmental toward others and can turn into bigotry, prejudice, and hatred.

Additionally, the problem with bias is it is reinforced through repeated usage, superstition, propaganda, and malice. We all have preferences. It is when those preferences cause or reinforce harm to others that they become exceedingly dangerous.

Bias is dangerous in any group or organization when there are power dynamics at play. We all want to be well thought of and fairly judged among our peers. When others' petty and unfounded preferences prevent us from success, cause our talents and those of others like us to be dismissed, and diminish our worth without regard for truth, bias can be catastrophic.

Those who might otherwise recognize and refrain from using bias to gain advantage may be tempted to do so, using differences to drive wedges to build scaffolding to stand upon as bully pulpits or even metaphorical gallows.

We see bias operate in museums when we wonder aloud why someone from a particular neighborhood or with a disability would ever want to visit a museum. We might assume that someone who lives in a certain zip code might not be able to afford a museum membership or might not enjoy the same kind of artistic pursuits or elements that others do. We might hold the assumptions that only certain cultures, or people with certain identities, enjoy math and science. These assumptions might unconsciously deny others the ability to visit or work in a science museum.

We might think we are applying critical thinking to a situation when, in fact, we are using bias to choose in favor of someone or something with more familiarity. A museum team might balk at budgeting for education programs for blind people if they refuse to believe that those who are blind might enjoy museum exhibitions too.

Bias might also be currying favor, expecting handouts, or thinking less of oneself and more of others because that is what have we been acculturated to think or believe.

We are not always aware of when we are using bias. In fact, we may also think we are unbiased when the biases are deeply engrained and apparent to everyone else but ourselves.

At the Inward stage of our DEAI interrogation, we should begin asking ourselves through journaling about the people or groups against whom we are biased and investigate why.

If we allow our biases to remain unchallenged, we create stereotypes that can become prejudices. These can turn into microaggressions toward others, resulting in outright bigoted conduct. Unchecked oppressive behavior contributes to an accepted bullying, unwelcoming culture.

Personal biases are the kind that make swift negative judgments about one's cleanliness based on the color of one's skin or the hairstyle worn. They're the kind that judge someone's surname as unacceptable for a leadership position because it might assume things about their language skills or lived experience. This kind of bias is compounded by ignorance and unfounded assumptions. Learning about others, developing compassion, practicing kindness, and revisiting impressions go a long way to challenging these assumptions.

We must first face what we intend to erase. Look closely. Look carefully. Acknowledge, accept, and then work to eradicate harmful biases.

IMPLICIT ASSOCIATION TEST

One helpful tool for identifying and assessing bias is the Implicit Association Test, or IAT.

Created at Project Implicit, a nonprofit and internationally partnered organization within Harvard University's campus, it is renowned for its keen ability to help identify and assess bias. This tool comprises a set of rapid prompts, photographs, and questions that measure response time to certain pairings of concepts and emotions. As you respond on a computer or mobile device to certain pictures or words, the results are measured in real time to provide an answer immediately following the experience.

The tool is available at no cost online, and those who take the assessment can choose which potential biases they would like to measure: skin color, race, gender, sexual orientation, religion, age, politics, and others.

For this exercise, please visit www.implicit.harvard.edu and follow the instructions. When you land on the page listing a variety of tests, select at least three but take as many as you can.

Write your responses to the IAT's results and your feedback about the process in your journal.

For an added exercise, complete these questions in your journal:

1. How did you feel while taking the IAT?
2. Were there any surprises that came up for you in the test or result?
3. Do you easily recognize that you have biases?

EXERCISE: REFLECTING ON MY BIASES, PART A

Please rate your agreement with the following statements on a scale of 1 to 5, where 1 is "Strongly Disagree" and 5 is "Strongly Agree."

1. I treat all individuals equally regardless of their race or ethnicity.

   1 2 3 4 5

2. I feel comfortable interacting with people from different cultures than my own.

   1 2 3 4 5

3. I have biases that I am aware of.

   1 2 3 4 5

4. I believe my biases influence my interactions with others.

   1 2 3 4 5

5. I try to challenge my own biases.

   1 2 3 4 5

6. I believe everyone has some form of bias.

   1 2 3 4 5

7. I believe that my biases do not affect my decision-making.

   1 2 3 4 5

8. I am open to learning about and understanding my own biases.

   1 2 3 4 5

9. I believe it's important to address and confront biases.

   1 2 3 4 5

10. My biases have changed over time.

   1 2 3 4 5

EXERCISE: REFLECTING ON MY BIASES, PART B

Please rate your agreement with the following statements on a scale of 1 to 5, where 1 is "Strongly Disagree" and 5 is "Strongly Agree."

1. I treat all museum visitors equally regardless of their race or ethnicity.

   1 2 3 4 5

2. I feel comfortable interacting with museum visitors from different cultures than my own.

   1 2 3 4 5

3. I have biases that I am aware of in my role as a museum employee.

   1 2 3 4 5

4. I think my biases influence my interactions with museum visitors.

   1 2 3 4 5

5. I try to challenge my own biases in my role as a museum employee.

   1 2 3 4 5

6. I believe everyone has some form of bias, including museum employees.

   1 2 3 4 5

7. I believe that my biases do not affect my decision-making in my role as a museum employee.

   1 2 3 4 5

8. I am open to learning about and understanding my own biases as a museum employee.

   1 2 3 4 5

9. I believe it's important to address and confront biases in the museum industry.

   1 2 3 4 5

10. I think that my biases have changed over time in my role as a museum employee.

    1 2 3 4 5

Expound on any of these feelings, thoughts, and beliefs in your journal.

DO THESE BIASES SHOW THEMSELVES IN YOUR MUSEUM?

Biases don't only function as levers that allow us to judge others consciously or unconsciously, resulting in name-calling or bad behavior. Bias does not always appear negative and sometimes can seem like simple preferences or choices. We are all entitled to our honest preferences and choices. That said, some organizations carefully construct biases into rules or preferred behaviors. When preferences have the effect of preventing certain viewpoints, individuals, or communities from holding space in a supposedly open and welcoming environment, one must wonder if those behaviors, policies, and practices aren't really just biases.

READ AND REFLECT

Respond to each of these statements with your opinion about whether these biases are visible in your museum from your vantage point as a leader, board member, staff member, volunteer, or other internal community member.

1. Lack of meaningful representation of marginalized communities in exhibitions and collections.
2. Lack of diverse perspectives in curatorial decision-making.
3. Limited interpretation of artworks or artifacts from non-Western cultures.
4. Limited knowledge of the names of nonwhite contributors to museum collections.
5. Stereotypical portrayals of certain cultures or communities in exhibits or programs.
6. Unequal access to resources and opportunities for marginalized museum professionals.
7. Tokenism, where only a few diverse voices or perspectives are included to create an appearance of diversity.
8. Exclusion of narratives or histories that challenge dominant narratives.
9. Limited representation of women artists or artists from LGBTQIA+ communities.
10. A disproportionate focus on European or Western art and history.
11. Biased language or descriptions in exhibition labels or educational materials.
12. A lack of accessibility for individuals with disabilities.
13. Pay disparities and inequitable treatment of museum staff based on gender, race, or other factors.
14. Limited engagement with local communities and their histories.
15. Inadequate recognition of indigenous knowledge and contributions.
16. Inequitable distribution of funding and resources among museums.
17. Lack of diversity in museum leadership and decision-making positions.
18. Incomplete or inaccurate historical narratives that downplay or ignore oppression.
19. Inconsistent representation of diverse perspectives in public programming and events.
20. Implicit bias in the selection and acquisition of artworks or artifacts.
21. Limited representation of artists or communities from low-income backgrounds.
22. Inadequate acknowledgment of the colonial origins of certain collections.
23. Insufficient efforts to repatriate or return stolen or looted artifacts to their rightful communities.
24. Biased treatment of visitors based on race, gender, or other factors.

25. Limited interpretation of controversial or challenging topics.
26. Lack of inclusive and accessible spaces for breastfeeding or prayer.
27. Inadequate representation of LGBTQIA+ histories and contributions.
28. Limited recognition of the contributions of people with disabilities in art and history.
29. Inequitable distribution of museum resources and programming across different neighborhoods or regions.
30. Hiring practices that favor certain backgrounds or educational institutions, particularly as seen in the language used in announcements, forms, and interviews.
31. Lack of diversity in museum boards and governing bodies.
32. Inadequate representation of the experiences of immigrants and refugees in the exhibits and programs.
33. Limited recognition of the contributions of women of color in art and history.
34. Inconsistent or biased treatment of artists or communities with controversial or dissenting views.
35. Limited interpretation of the impact of colonization on indigenous communities.
36. Inequitable representation of different religions and spiritual practices.
37. Biased portrayal of certain historical figures or events.
38. Limited recognition of the contributions of people from different socioeconomic backgrounds.
39. Inadequate representation of the experiences of people with mental health challenges.
40. Biased interpretation of scientific or natural history exhibits.
41. Limited recognition of the contributions of people from different regions or countries.
42. Inequitable representation of different ethnic or racial groups.
43. Biased interpretation of the contributions of women in science and technology.
44. Limited recognition of the contributions of people from different political or ideological backgrounds.
45. Inadequate representation of the experiences of people from different generations.
46. Biased interpretation of the impact of historic enslavement and racial discrimination.
47. Limited recognition of the contributions of people from different religious or spiritual backgrounds.
48. Inequitable representation of different social or cultural movements.
49. Biased interpretation of the impact of war and conflict.
50. Limited recognition of the contributions of people from different linguistic backgrounds.

51. Inadequate representation of the experiences of people from different family structures or relationship types.

Have you ever noticed any of these cultural norms in museums in general or in your specific museum? Have you tended to contribute to, fortify, or champion any of these norms, which are based on biases? Thankfully, the field is slowly changing as individuals, work teams, museum associations, and governing bodies revisit their previously exclusionary and biased practices. It starts with individuals. How do you help your museum as peer groups, departmental groups, staff groups, and leaders to do the same?

We have to live what we preach so that the lessons will take root and thrive. Merely telling one person with more authority that a policy is actually biased or imagining that your suggestion to be more inclusive will someday make it become the new policy for the institution is not realistic. Another reason to write down your thoughts is to practice using your own powers and privileges, beginning with the powers to read, write, cognize, and think critically. These were privileges denied the ancestors of many still-marginalized people today. In oppressive environments, leaders often forbid those who are experiencing hardship to write their experiences down. In some museums, the unspoken, often biased and polarizing rules are the same ones as the unwritten rules. These remnants of colonizer thinking are not accidental.

EXERCISE: I AM, BUT I AM NOT

Think about your identities. Are there some that are stronger than others? Do you feel more affinity toward one than the other for whatever reason? How do others feel about one or more of your identities? Do others make assumptions about you because of your characteristics, identities, orientation, religion, or other markers?

Complete the following table, naming or describing your characteristic or identity, then stating a quality you don't possess but others might still think about you due to their bias or assumptions. The first is an example already filled out for you.

EXERCISE: I FEEL, I THINK, I BELIEVE

This exercise is important to help you separate your emotions from opinions and fact.

In colloquial speech, one might use the phrase "I feel" when what they actually mean is "I think." For example, somebody might say "I feel like people are too argumentative these days," when they really mean they feel annoyed, sad, or unhappy that people are too argumentative and they think people are too argumentative too.

I am short	But I am not a child

When we allow ourselves to feel and accept the initial emotions we are experiencing, we can be even more descriptive, aware, and voluble about the situation at hand.

Similarly, to use the terms "think" and "believe" interchangeably is to miss a subtle but important difference in potency. A thought is more ephemeral than a belief. Beliefs have more power. Actions are born of beliefs.

For this exercise, respond to each of the following statements by stating what you feel, think, or believe. Following is an example:

Museums are overcrowded and don't provide access to visitors.
a. I feel sad about this.
b. I think museums can problem-solve to reduce crowding.
c. I believe museums are still important.

1. Museums say they are welcoming to children but have an atmosphere that reads hands off.

    a. I feel_____.
    b. I think_____.
    c. I believe_____.

2. Museums never support emerging artists; they always go with the already famous.

    a. I feel_____.
    b. I think_____.
    c. I believe_____.

3. Museums take advantage of their volunteers and interns by not paying them.

    a. I feel_____.
    b. I think_____.
    c. I believe_____.

4. Museums are becoming obsolete in a digital world.

    a. I feel_____.
    b. I think_____.
    c. I believe_____.

5. All museums should be free of charge to enter, just like public libraries.

    a. I feel_____.
    b. I think_____.
    c. I believe_____.

MUSEUMS AND ME

Museums are among the kinds of institutions in the United States of America that maintain a sense of elegance, mystery, and prestige. It can be exhilarating for those who thrive in sumptuous surroundings from a certain aesthetic. Others may find these sorts of spaces stuffy and pretentious. Those who like to collect objects and those who like regimentation and order are also those who find museums appealing. The relationship between humans and objects, written communication and visual communication, art, and spatial communication is important to museology and a fascination for those in the field. Interpretation, storytelling, imagination, and creativity are all hallmarks of quality museums as well.

1. Why am I drawn to museums?
2. What other kinds of entertainment or educational experiences do I enjoy?
3. Do I like the direction museums are headed?
4. What can I do to help diversify museums?
5. What can I do to encourage others who don't want museums to change?

3

The Individual and the 21st-Century Museum

HOW MUSEUMS HAVE CHANGED AND WHY INDIVIDUALS
NEED TO ADAPT

WHO BELONGS IN A MUSEUM?

Museums feel like home for some people but not for others. For some people, museums are bright, beautiful bastions of culture, the art and artifacts of which were looted, plundered, stolen, or hoarded by those of immense power and privilege. They showcase brilliant jewels and celebrate the thieves who stole them for caprice and status.

It is not by accident that for the hundreds of years since museums have been formally present in the United States until very recently, the focus of major collections has been culturally Eurocentric, with the art makers or historical figures of note being white men of European descent, also predominantly straight and Christian. Stacked side by side with similar institutions, there are parallels in terms of the benefactors, contributors, rule makers, shareholders, stakeholders, and beneficiaries. The fields of higher education, the medical complex, and federal government have all historically been governed by a white male majority.

Those who enjoy a favorable status quo with its attendant benefits will do what it takes to uphold and defend that status quo at any cost unless they are faced with a higher prerogative and will to share or cede that power.

In a country where, within many of our lifetimes, it has taken decades of campaigns, marches, protests, legislation, and even loss of life for people of different races to simply sip water from the same drinking fountain, it's no wonder that the deeply striated system established centuries ago should persist and prevail.

I remember hearing someone chuckle when I mentioned how healthy it could be for people of color to state that they loved their cultural heritage. A young team member responded when I asked him to explain his reaction: "Dude, who would want to be Black?"

In recent years, there has been a push to examine museums' historical roles in Western exploitation, colonization, and oppression of minoritized communities as well as their continued intentional and unintentional preservation of the status quo.

As law, science, and culture have resolved to recognize different viewpoints and perspectives with compassion in an information age, museum funders, boards, and donors are becoming more accepting of DEAI imperatives.

Cyber technology's wide reach as an accountability tool and communication device has become a necessary driver in this charge. Technology is considered democratic, with its wide reach in information sharing, but not everyone has the hardware necessary to harness these powers because it is still too expensive and unaffordable for many adults and children.

Museum models before the 21st century prioritized the notion that museums were experts and museum workers labored under that conceit. They had the knowledge, and the hoi polloi would approach them with complete trust and belief that what they were displaying or teaching was accurate, important, well researched, and universal.

Museums are in service of the communities that surround them, both internal and external.

Cabinets of curiosity have existed for thousands of years, as humans have always felt the need to collect, to muse, to name, to describe, and to honor. The communities, clans, and countries that amassed and housed these treasures used various methods to collect what they deemed valuable.

A brief history of museums in the United States of America reveals parallels of the highly fraught social, economic, political, and cultural systems of the last four hundred years as they grew into and fought to become a country. The native peoples they exploited and decimated and the enslaved African people they purchased as heavy machinery and household appliances had absolutely no say in the founding of any of these systems; for that matter, neither did many other Americans to varying degrees. Yet for the Native American tribes and the enslaved Africans, their cultural products and valued spiritual objects were trivialized, misunderstood, misrepresented, mishandled, and maligned. The labor of their hands became bagatelles and trinkets for wry humor and fascination.

The Exotic Other was not relegated to Black and Indigenous either. As collections from the Middle East, Asia, and North Africa started to proliferate North American museums, the objects' representation, interpretation, and contextualization were done solely through a Western lens. Comparisons of style and method between a Western and so-called Oriental artwork would always yield a judgment of childlike, exotic, othered, and inferior.

Practices like these disregarded the complexities of cultures and maximized stereotypical portrayals of precious talent, time, and makers.

We see the august halls of early American museums of the mid- to late 19th century, and we think of the robber barons who funded them, families who supported them, and treasures that filled them. There's an even uglier side to museums as other, related institutions captivated Americans' spirits. The traveling circus, the expositions, and the zoological gardens were developing alongside them.

One of the saddest stories that comes out of this not-too-distant historical time—in the century in which I was born—was the story of Ota Benga. He was a Congolese man who was brought to the United States in 1904 as a collection item as a captured human, at about nineteen years of age. He was to be classified and exhibited as a "pygmy"—a living example of a so-called primitive culture.

Ota Benga was first exhibited at the St. Louis World Fair in 1904. The exhibit was so successful that he was next taken to the Bronx Zoo in New York City, where he was displayed in the Monkey House with the primates. Ota Benga was subjected to humiliating, degrading treatment in the cage, forced to wear only a loincloth, and told to act in ways that vilely reinforced racist tropes and stereotypes.

After two years of outrage and public pressure levied by African American clergymen and a few other human rights activists, Ota Benga was finally freed and went to live with an African American community in Virginia. Sadly, depression, ignominy, isolation, memory, and prejudice were his constant companions and perpetual plagues. In 1916, Benga took his own life.

This tragic story encapsulates the relationship museums and their ilk have had and continue to have with their audiences and stakeholders even to this day. Exploitation and discrimination loom large still. Thankfully, there are museum ethics in place to obviate another such harrowing, tragic story.

Despite civil rights action, legislation, the will of good people, and deep desire, it's difficult for some museums to disabuse themselves of the notion of the Exotic Other.

MORE ANTI-BIAS REFLECTION

As museum practitioners working together, we must help each other become our best selves by intentionally working on our common goal together. It's hard to confront our biases in private, much less to have dialogical experiences.

Let us consider that bias isn't just thinking about or acting inappropriately toward people or groups we don't like or may not even realize we don't like!

Here are ten kinds of bias and examples of how they insidiously operate. Which ones do you find yourself and others in your museum using unwittingly?

Common Classification of Biases and How They Are Expressed in Museums

Name	Definition	Generic Example 1	Generic Example 2	Specific Example from Your Museum
Affinity Bias	Favoring people who remind you of yourself or others with whom you have a rapport or affinity.	When selecting a candidate for employment, you go directly to someone who reminds you of yourself as a younger career person.	A curator is inclined to select someone they get along with who attended their university instead of selecting an artist of color who has never had a solo show.	
Anchoring Bias	The tendency to overly rely on a single piece of information or the first pieces of information presented.	Museum staff rely on exhibition feedback from the early days of the exhibition's run instead of ensuring that data is collected throughout the duration.	Museum staff prioritize artwork that has received significant media attention or critical acclaim.	

Name	Definition	Generic Example 1	Generic Example 2	Specific Example from Your Museum
Attribution Bias	Dominant identities (Straight, White, Male, Christian, able bodied) or valued entities (prominent, respected organizations) receive more credit for their accomplishments and less blame for their mistakes.	Museum leadership attributes the positive attention given the current exhibition to the museum's reputation rather than the hard work and quality of the exhibition staff and curators.	Education staff attribute the lack of visitor engagement with an exhibit program to the audience's lack of education and interest rather than considering the effectiveness and relevance of that program.	
Beauty Bias (also called "lookism")	A bias that leads to discrimination or prejudice based on a person's physical appearance, giving favor if the person conforms to society's standards of attractiveness. It may also include factors such as weight, height, skin color, facial features, hair texture, and body shape.	Museum personnel who are seen by human resources and other leaders at the institution as more conventionally attractive get called on to do more outward-facing activities, many of which are more attractive special opportunities that lead to enhanced connections and promotions.	At a museum donor event, a table of curators and directors in conversation is heard talking about plastic surgery and, in particular, encouraging a colleague to remove facial wrinkles despite her refusal in order to look "better for the museum's sake."	

(continued)

Name	Definition	Generic Example 1	Generic Example 2	Specific Example from Your Museum
Contrast Effect	A bias that evaluates similar people or characteristics against each other rather than on their own unique merits.	The museum hiring committee, being inundated with résumés, thins the stack by arbitrarily comparing similar-seeming résumés against each other and selecting one via random or impossibly high standards.	Theo, a regular museum visitor, was incredibly impressed with an expensive, highly interactive exhibition that the museum displayed that past summer. The subsequent smaller, less flashy exhibitions were not viewed by him as successful or interesting even though they were well curated and designed.	
Gender Bias	Bias, or preference, for one gender over others. Gender bias can cause someone to unwittingly favor someone based on stereotypical characteristics assigned to someone who identifies as a man, a woman, agender, bigender, genderfluid, genderqueer, or other genders.	The museum has not hired a female preparator in its history because "getting up on a ladder and hammering nails into the wall is men's work."	The board of directors believes that cisgender men make the best museum directors and ask questions during informal meetings during a weeks-long interview process to determine how conforming the individual is to that norm.	

Name	Definition	Generic Example 1	Generic Example 2	Specific Example from Your Museum
Halo Effect	This bias notices and fixates on an individual's (or thing's) positive remarkable trait and can see no wrong because that single overshadowing characteristic makes them seem exceptional.	The museum's new chief curator is an Ivy League graduate but is a terrible manager with a sour personality and is an inconsistent employee and marginally good at his job.	The museum shop sells beautiful jewelry made by a celebrity jeweler whose work is featured on a popular television show. Although the shop needs to make room for local artists and other kinds of designs, they keep showcasing the designs of the celebrity even when her work is subpar.	
Horns Effect	This bias notices and fixates on an individual's (or thing's) negative remarkable trait and can see no wrong because that single overshadowing characteristic makes them seem unacceptable.	A massive scandal overtook the museum, and the disgraced CEO was canceled. Several funders and donors withdrew support, and the museum's popularity severely and suddenly declined.	A family visiting the museum is ignored at the admissions desk, and they feel slighted. Eventually, as they make their way through the museum, they see nothing good or noteworthy in the exhibitions and have a terrible time.	

Affinity Bias. Copyright 2023 Sam Day. *Used with permission, created for Cecile Shellman Consulting.*

Anchoring Bias. *Copyright 2023 Sam Day. Used with permission, created for Cecile Shellman Consulting.*

Attribution Bias. *Copyright 2023 Sam Day. Used with permission, created for Cecile Shellman Consulting.*

Beauty Bias. *Copyright 2023 Sam Day. Used with permission, created for Cecile Shellman Consulting.*

Contrast Effect. *Copyright 2023 Sam Day. Used with permission, created for Cecile Shellman Consulting.*

Gender Bias. *Copyright 2023 Sam Day. Used with permission, created for Cecile Shellman Consulting.*

Halo Bias. *Copyright 2023 Sam Day. Used with permission, created for Cecile Shellman Consulting.*

Horns Effect. *Copyright 2023 Sam Day. Used with permission, created for Cecile Shellman Consulting.*

Part II
Outward

4

Working with Others toward a Common Goal in the Museum

As museum employees, staff, volunteers, leadership, and others, self-assess and give themselves the grace and permission to ask and answer challenging prompts about their origin stories, biases, and conflict resolution strategies, they may develop curiosity about how their peers respond to the same questions.

Conversations that happen under the imprimatur of shared understanding and in service of a shared outcome can be fortifying, intimate, and extraordinary. Courageous conversations about polarizing ideas; personal attributes and beliefs; cultural proficiency; bias and oppression; power and privilege—these can happen in museum workspaces, too, despite the tensions and turmoil that sometimes pervade the work environment.

Museum culture—the way museums are and how museum people behave—is a culture that values perfection, symmetry, order, and authority. As museum practitioners, we tend to feel safe when there is calmness and confidence. I understand the fear that people feel when a workshop about cultural competence, racial justice, disability awareness, and anti-oppression is about to occur. It can feel unsafe. It can feel unmoored and daunting. Some of us feel scared as though we shouldn't be doing this at all or in public. Some of the very values that built the museum complex are the ones we are charged to tear apart brick by brick, and not everyone is on board.

Readiness, internal fortitude, and capacity are the careful considerations that should be taken when helming an interactive DEAI approach. What is your work culture like? How do you get along with each other? How do you handle conflict? Who is already on board, and who needs to be cajoled? Whose values are diametrically opposed? What strategies can we offer for buy-in?

A WORD ABOUT DEAI PROGRAM LEADERS

If we are to understand cultures, ways of being, people, and communities different from ourselves whom we are not serving adequately, we need to first understand ourselves as colleagues.

The next, concurrent stage of work in our DEAI engagement is to learn and grow together through team building, in service, professional development, workshops, enhanced staff meetings, scheduled formal conversations, and employee resource groups.

If the individual journaling assignments have stalled or if it might help to have reminders to the larger group, the DEAI working group could help arrange accountability partnerships: pairings among staff members to encourage each other to complete assigned exercises or readings.

Depending on staff cultural norms, the frequency and style of planned meetings could change as appropriate. If the working group plans most of the meetings in concert with the senior leadership team of the museum, the topics they work on will be more substantive than if they are working by themselves.

We talk in terms of similarities and differences when we discuss culture. If we make uninformed guesses about people who are different from us, we bear the risk of reinforcing prejudices that are broad, stereotypical, and untrue. When an entity, such as a museum, and individuals, such as its staff and leadership, get culture wrong, the result can be catastrophic.

We have to work with others in real time to learn about and from each other. We can consume social media, watch television around the clock, read all the best-selling books, and listen to award-winning podcasts, but if we don't get together in real time, we will miss social cues and the opportunity to bond as friends.

Despite our nation's pluralistic composition, there are many locales around the country that have never experienced much diversity. Since unity and collegiality don't appear to be problematic for them, they conclude it must not really be the problem for anyone, and they deny the need to join the rest of the field in practicing how to build diversity and welcoming strategies. Culture is more than looks, however. A community that has a homogeneous racial or ethnic composition may experience great diversity in religions, which may affect how some of the population may experience or treat gender or sexual orientation-based minorities.

We need to practice talking among ourselves to strengthen relationships and give ourselves permission to gently make mistakes, to reduce embarrassment, practice forgiveness, use humor in ways that do not cause harm, and practice compassion.

When I read anonymous caustic social media takedowns of allegedly barbaric, racist, homophobic, or otherwise clueless leadership actions at museums by their own staff, I admit that I wonder a little about whether their internal culture invited authentic discussion, community, and comradery. If museums are all truthfully grappling together with their own humanity, learning to trust each other and care about each other along the way, less of these poisonous, punitive challenges would be had. This is not to say that many of these gripes aren't well deserved or that the egregious behavior should not be addressed. With dialogue and introspection, honesty, and transparency, some of the corrections can be made closer to the center, with more impact and less shame. At the core, powerless people may believe that calling out and cancellation are their only tools of transformation. Introspection and working as teams to address problems first might be more workable solutions. Working together will also reveal to everyone the true character of those helming the organization, and empowered, informed decisions can then be made.

As we create opportunities to dialogue with each other in museums, we should be prepared to accept the following:

- Not everyone will want to engage in anti-oppression work, but we all must give our best effort.
- Whether because of shyness, skepticism, or displeasure, those who do not care to participate may try to make things more difficult for the team players by responding sarcastically, giving fake answers, or laughing uncomfortably to defuse the seriousness of the moment. At the beginning of every shared dialogue session, read aloud a set of norms for behaving while in a brave and safe space. Add your own norms if needed. Hold everyone to account.
- Time must be allocated to hold regular discussions about DEAI among the staff. It's not enough to produce one or two daylong all-staff training workshops every year, difficult as even that may be to achieve. If we are serious about the nature of the work, the gravity demands the weight of a constant force.

It may take the shape of large-scale all-hands-on-deck gatherings, frequent casual huddles, agenda items in every (yes, every) staff meeting, quotations and provocative queries in the break room, a lending library, and suggested podcast listening sessions. The main idea is to create opportunities to gather and give specific permission to the staff to speak freely about what they observe and experience.

Staff members and volunteers may begin to feel friendly and trusting enough to share some of their most interesting epiphanies about themselves, their identities and culture, or the museum.

The themes build from who you are and what you are capable of as individuals to what you can do and what you are capable of together.

We are not interchangeable. Each of us matters. If museums are going to change, each museum needs to reckon and grapple together, exploring what they know and what they believe, talking honestly with and among and about themselves to understand what they want and what they can handle in terms of change.

Readiness doesn't just mean financial status and real estate resources, such as office space or a shiny new elevator.

Who is in place at the leadership level at the time? What are their values and beliefs? Do they have the power to effect change officially, unofficially, or potentially?

What kind of privilege do they possess? Do they realize that privilege is also a power?

COMMON GOAL: SERVING OTHERS

To that end, if we believe and behave as if one's DEAI effort can yield justice on the other side of the equation, it will.

DEAI done for its own sake is a checklist of activities that have/hold no lasting resonance.

I remember when I was in graduate school and had as a term assignment the development of my very own exhibition. I was an older student who had worked on a few exhibitions myself in other organizations and capacities. I was sure that I knew how to do this, that I did not need much assistance, and that I could sail through the project with a high grade without too much effort.

I was sorely disappointed during my first meeting with my professor. She called my exhibit idea unilateral and trite. The design was too simple. The concept was lacking. I was surprised at this but soon understood the value of multiple viewpoints. I learned how to value feedback and to respect the voice of expertise.

Sometimes in departmental teams, we like to work in silos and are competitive with other departments in our museum. There is no need. We can work much better when we are collaborative and gain insight from each other, In fact, it's a decolonizing practice to work across the organization.

CEDING POWER

Examining self is only the first stage in a justice-focused initiative where the goal is for individuals and the groups to which they belong to work authentically to use their power to change. Power is a privilege, and everyone in a museum organization has some access to power on one level or another. Those with more power have more responsibility to effect change. There are higher expectations and more scrutiny.

Power can be organizational, authoritarian, positional, or referent. If power is used to facilitate, rather than to control, healthy boundaries can be established, leading to positive change and respect for each other.

Whenever we work with others, we open ourselves up to comparison and examine our relationships with the power brokers with whom we interact.

I have worked with and for some brilliant, perceptive, kind bosses who were honestly intent on mentoring their staff and doing good in the world. I worked with others who too easily fell prey to the maxim "Power corrupts, and absolute power corrupts absolutely."

Those with the most power in a system may believe they have earned the right to behave in entitled ways, constantly drawing attention to their superior status, showing more fascination for their positions than for the jobs they were hired to execute, and expecting unrealistic perfection in others. There are many museums that are helmed by visionary, caring leaders, but even then, when there are systems and patterns built on oppression and prejudice, what seems normal is actually unnecessary and sometimes harmful. When a director has an entire suite of offices, some with more square footage than the average home, and employees are sat desk to desk in cramped windowless workrooms, that's a problem.

All departments within a museum should be prepared to work together for the ultimate goals of anti-oppression and justice within its walls, among its stakeholders, and in their communities.

There are many kinds of museums, from zoos to historical houses, art museums, and science centers. Art museums are the most numerous, seconded by historic sites and history museums, then science museums, children's museums, zoos, and aquariums. There are museums without walls, including technological museums, some residing entirely online. There are geographically dispersed museums and museums that operate out of a home or small business office. A museum may be an ancestral home or an occupied house chock full of delightful ephemera; amusing novelties; and sacred, fun, or homemade items. They may have widely accessible viewing hours or may be open once a month on a Sunday. Some museums strive for accreditation and adhere to the strictures of a governing body. Others are museums as a viable business model but do their own thing.

In this next section, I'll describe an approach museums can take to begin to work together cross departmentally. The example may not apply to all museums or all circumstances. Where possible, apply the principles you can to your current circumstances and museum model. The departments described may be departments of three or departments of one or may not even exist in your area or organization. If this is the case, explore the questions following this section to see which employees or volunteers perform the functions described and consider whether inter-museum collaboration would be probable. Even within more traditional models, realize that governance, titles of positions or departments, and behaviors may differ.

A TYPICAL MUSEUM ORGANIZATION CHART AND SUGGESTIONS FOR WORKING CROSS DEPARTMENTALLY

1. Curatorial

   - Curator: Responsible for selecting and organizing collections, conducting research, and developing exhibitions. Some zoos, science museums, and historic houses also have curators even though the term *curator* is primarily used in art museums. In some cases, the curator may even be the director, and the department may comprise one or two people. In other museums, this may be one of the largest departments.
   - Collections Manager: Oversees the management and preservation of collections, including acquisition, cataloging, and conservation.
   - Registrar: Manages the documentation, inventory, and legal aspects of museum collections.

2. Education Department

   - Director of Education/Educator: Leads the concept development of the interpretive programs and oversees department staff.
   - Education Coordinator/Educator: Develops and implements educational programs, tours, workshops, and activities for visitors, students, and community groups.
   - Outreach Coordinator: Organizes museum outreach efforts to schools, community centers, and other organizations.
   - Interpretation Specialist: Creates interpretive materials, labels, and multimedia displays to enhance visitor experiences.

3. Exhibition Design and Development Department

   - Exhibition Designer: Designs and plans the visual design, physical layout, displays, and interactive elements of exhibitions, usually with an internal or contracted team of designers.
   - Graphic Designer: Creates visual graphics, signage, and promotional materials.
   - Audiovisual Technician: Installs and maintains audiovisual equipment for exhibitions and multimedia displays.
   - Exhibition Technician: Assists with the fabrication, installation, and maintenance of exhibit components. Sometimes this position is a contracted position outside the museum or might be the purview of the physical facilities department or individual responsible for maintenance.
   - Lighting Technician: Designs and sets up lighting systems for optimal exhibition viewing and maintains museum standards to protect the art and artifacts. In some cases, this is not a required or necessary position or may be relevant on an exhibition-by-exhibition basis.

4. Visitor Services Department

   - Front Desk/Reception: Greets visitors, sells tickets, provides orientation information to guests, and handles general inquiries.
   - Museum Guide/Docent: Conducts tours, educates visitors about exhibits, and provides basic knowledge about the museum's collections. Some museums have all-volunteer museum guides and/or docents, and their positions are primarily unpaid. Some are included in the budget and receive monetary compensation.
   - Visitor Services Manager: Oversees frontline staff and ensures positive visitor experiences.

5. Marketing and Communications Department

   - Marketing Manager: Develops marketing strategies, promotions, and advertising campaigns to attract visitors and increase awareness of museum events.
   - Public Relations Officer: Builds relationships with the media, handles press releases, and manages media coverage.
   - Social Media Coordinator: Manages the museum's social media presence and engages with online audiences.
   - Graphic Designer: Creates visual materials for marketing and advertising purposes.

6. Development/Fundraising Department

   - Development Manager/Officer: Plans and executes fundraising initiatives for the museum, seeks grants, and manages donor relations.
   - Membership Coordinator: Administers membership programs, cultivates member relationships, and manages member benefits.

7. Operations and Facilities Department

   - Facility Manager: Oversees the maintenance, security, and infrastructure of the museum building and grounds.
   - Operations Coordinator: Manages logistics, budgets, and scheduling for events, programs, and exhibitions.

8. Technology

   - IT Specialist: Supports and maintains computer systems, networks, and digital platforms used by the museum.

9. Gift Shop Staff
10. Human Resources/Payroll/Bursar/Financial Services

Large museums will typically also have a separate human resources department.

A checklist-focused approach to integrating DEAI into the museum's offerings might be to create a list of to-dos for each department to check off on their own.

The position of senior DEAI officer should occupy the same organizational position as a high leader in the museum, whether that be president or vice president, reporting to the executive director, director, or chief executive officer.

An interdepartmental approach would require thoughtful, long-term planning and team building across museum divisions.

Looking at the work across museums and lining up the priorities against the strategic plan, a museum may find that its main activities are as follows:

- Displaying exhibitions (about six per year)
- Designing exhibitions for in-house display (about one per year)
- Raising funds to support museum activities and operations
- Promoting exhibitions and programs
- Training docents and interns

A skilled, invested director of DEAI can help each department convene to discuss their intersections and how to weave diversity, equity, accessibility, and inclusion into each stage of the project planning.

DEPARTMENT WORK VERSUS INTRADEPARTMENTAL WORK

One of the best, most instructive experiences of my museum work life was participating in two major exhibition development projects as a museum education staff member in the late 1990s at the Museum of Church History and Art in Salt Lake City. As an education curator, I was asked to co-curate a children's exhibition with a lead curator and take part in its highly collaborative museum development project. The museum's development schedule was planned three to five years in advance, and every step was carefully mapped out well before year 1 commenced. This cycle allowed several exhibitions to be planned at the same time.

A museum-wide DEAI initiative should facilitate all departments working together on each other's primary projects.

Collaboration among all departments and auxiliaries—the museum gift shop, physical facilities, operations, curators, fundraisers, and education department—is crucial for the success of an exhibition. Here are some ways they can work together over the course of a year to support the exhibition:

1. Initial Planning Phase
   - Curators and the education department collaborate to define the exhibition's theme, objectives, and educational goals.

- Fundraisers work with curators to identify potential funding sources and develop a fundraising strategy.
- The gift shop team researches and identifies relevant merchandise that aligns with the exhibition's theme and can be sold to support the exhibition financially.

2. Exhibition Development Phase

- Curators and the education department work closely to select artworks, artifacts, or exhibits that align with the exhibition's theme and educational goals.
- The gift shop team collaborates with curators to develop merchandise that complements the exhibition and appeals to visitors.
- Fundraisers actively seek funding opportunities, including grants, sponsorships, and donations, to support the exhibition's development and related educational programs.

3. Exhibition Design and Installation Phase

- Curators and the education department provide input on the exhibition design, ensuring it aligns with the intended narrative and educational objectives.
- The gift shop team collaborates with exhibition designers to create a visually appealing and engaging retail space within the exhibition area.
- Fundraisers continue to seek additional funding to support the exhibition's design, installation, and related educational initiatives.

4. Exhibition Promotion and Public Engagement

- The education department develops educational programs, workshops, and guided tours that enhance visitors' understanding of the exhibition's themes.
- The gift shop team promotes exhibition-related merchandise through marketing campaigns, ensuring visitors are aware of the available products.
- Fundraisers work with the marketing team to promote the exhibition and its associated fundraising initiatives, encouraging donations and sponsorships.

5. Ongoing Support and Evaluation

- The education department continues to offer educational programs and events throughout the exhibition's duration, collaborating with curators to ensure alignment with the exhibition's content.
- The gift shop team regularly updates and refreshes merchandise to maintain visitor interest and generate revenue to support the exhibition.

- Fundraisers evaluate the success of fundraising efforts, identify areas for improvement, and continue seeking funding opportunities to sustain the exhibition and related programs.

Regular communication, coordination, and shared goals among these departments are essential for a successful exhibition. By working together, they can enhance the visitor experience, generate revenue, and support the exhibition's development, education, and long-term sustainability.

How much more important, then, is it for the tenets of diversity, equity, accessibility, justice, anti-oppression, pro-BIPOC, anti-bias, repatriation, Afro-futurism, and others to be thoroughly discussed and planned for at every level of the museum development activity?

QUESTIONS FOR SMALL MUSEUMS, LESS-TRADITIONAL MUSEUMS, AND OTHERS

1. Answer for yourself as an individual and with small pairs or groups if possible or relevant:

   a. When you encounter new museum theories or suggestions that could propel your DEAI ideas forward, do you feel overwhelmed because of your personnel size, budget, or time constraints?
   b. Are there opportunities for you to connect with like-minded and similarly situated museums to share resources, co-work, or collaborate virtually to stimulate new thought and generate support?
   c. How can you realistically work with your team members if there are few opportunities due to time, distance, and other factors?
   d. Realizing that technology can be both boon and barrier, how can you apply the use of workplace technological tools, social media, and design thinking to collaborating on your DEAI-focused planning?

2. If you are a small team or even a team of one, find trustworthy accountability partners to confide in regarding your values and principles about diversity, equity, accessibility, inclusion, anti-oppression, pro-BIPOC, and pro-marginalized people's concerns.

5

When Beliefs and Actions Collide

DEALING WITH CONFLICT AND MICROAGGRESSIONS

As an advanced Spanish speaker and Portuguese language learner I came across an interesting fact in a Brazilian documentary: People who live on the Brazilian/Paraguayan border speak a hybrid language called Portunhol. The portmanteau was coined to describe the patois itself, a mélange of Portuguese (portuguese) and Spanish (español). An interviewee recounted that when he first heard Portuguese even as an adult, he had no idea there was even a language called Portuguese: He believed, instead, that those he was hearing say seemingly similar words to Spanish ones probably had speech delays or cognitive disabilities. The majority of the South American continent speaks Spanish. Without additional knowledge, this Paraguayan and other Spanish speakers could have ignored, become frustrated with, and dismissed the community members on the Borderlands. Speaking Portunhol allows people to communicate serviceably among themselves to the extent they wish and in pursuit of their common goals.

I liken this kludge to what happens in a work environment: In a workplace, people with various identities and numerous cultures and from various home traditions meet daily to labor for a specific purpose. To achieve the organization's goals, communication is the highest priority, and, therefore, learning a new workable tailor-made skill might even be called for to share the journey toward that successful objective. Whatever it takes, we must work together. Conflict in any relationship is a reality. Meeting in the middle, being creative to solve problems, and having a sense a humor along the way will aid in supporting a healthy company culture.

We don't necessarily join a workplace to become friends or to gain individual fame and fortune. We work because we have something to contribute to the cause and support the objective at hand. In museums, that objective has been to conceive, design, present, and share exhibitions of art, nature, science, or history to the public.

You endure fracases at work, as there are anywhere imperfect people gather, because in our professional culture we know not to spin out too far. We don't say the kinds of things or behave in the same ways we do toward our personal friends and family to decelerate conflict because we don't have as much invested in those relationships. When our money is on the line, we tend to keep our emotions more in check.

Even so, because we are human and our work structures remain colonized and still bear vestiges of harmful work patterns and oppressive behaviors, there is bound to be friction, misery, and pain at work. We will still be involved in many abrasive interactions, some of which we'll tamp down to save face and retain our professional demeanors. Unfortunately, this can contribute to a hostile work culture over time.

From Glassdoor.com come these abysmal reviews that demonstrate the kinds of conflict that persist in museum culture:

> Poor pay, inexperienced and extremely out of touch leadership has led to gross mismanagement, unhappy and overtaxed workers, and an alarming turnover rate. Management knows that because of the allure of museum work there is always another young, eager worker ready to jump in and take someone's job and they hold this as a threat over a number of workers' heads. It's a true shame.

> Sadness is the main emotion of staff. Every staff member loathes the institution, so meetings and conversations devolve into complaining almost instantly. Management is aware but does nothing to course correct staff morale. Great work is not celebrated. Curators rule; accessibility of programs comes second. Pretentious. This cannot be overstated. Zero engagement with community and ignorance of 21st-century relevance.

> Senior leadership is toxic and treats smart and passionate staff members like obstructions rather than allies and collaborators. Arrogance, privilege, and condescension run rampant among a management team that lacks intellectual depth, leadership experience, and empathy.

> The board is more of a vanity project for the wealthy looking to gain insight on their next art purchase and/or to maintain their status in affluent social circles.
> Diversity of staff is another glaring weakness. As long as the museum is run by the same revolving door of elitist white people who come from privilege, no real change can or will occur.

Yet these are workplaces that ostensibly support DEAI initiatives. What's happening?

When it comes to matters of diversity, equity, accessibility, inclusion, justice, and belonging, things can become very personal very quickly. There are not many other places, times, or circumstances where we are regularly asked to divulge feelings or thoughts about our own or others' behavior and characteristics. It may be embarrassing to admit among ourselves that we have biases against other people, some of whom are in the same room.

Some museum workers feel a need to act out the Downton Abbey–style drama of catering to or being the financially powerful while the ones who do the physical labor are given too much to do for too little money and praise and have little freedom. Contrary to the opinions of some, museums are not only for white, wealthy, able-bodied people. The systems of privilege will persist if they are not intentionally upended.

In a workplace, we may not like our coworkers' or supervisors' personalities or behavior, but we soldier on. If we want to keep our jobs and have the leaders think well of us, we sometimes have to behave contrary to our nature. If someone bothers or insults us, we have to quickly forgive or pretend we did. Tempering our feelings is more difficult to accomplish when we are asked to think and talk about culture, identity, interpersonal relationships, and behavioral change on an ongoing basis and as we learn more and more about each other. Ideally, we should have empathy for each other and draw closer, learning how to trust each other along the way. However, real life doesn't always operate in this manner.

In workplaces where diversity and inclusion are stressed, there are sometimes fears by the current staff members concerning their own job safety. Negative feelings about people of color, people who are from low socioeconomic status, and other people who seek jobs in the museum industry may be pervasive in the organization because of personal bias, bigotry, a scarcity mindset, and lack of clarity about lawful hiring practices.

Ultimately, there will be new recruits and employees in the workplace. Museums that were once so white are diversifying in terms of race and ethnicity. They are also more accepting of people with disabilities, sexual and gender minorities, and people whose first language is not English.

In this kind of environment, microaggressions will creep up and flourish due to our hidden biases and our illusion that if we don't talk about difficult things, they disappear. As museum workers, we are often admired and even envied, but we also know the sting of snide comments about our chosen industry—that we don't have a real job, looking at art all day; that we deal in soft sciences and pretend education and, therefore, our work is not as rigorous; that we are not true professionals but simply entertainment brokers. These comments hurt. They are similar to microaggressions, but microaggressions have an even more distinct tenor.

Microaggressions are particular sorts of behaviors or comments that communicate negative messages toward people based on their cultural characteristics or identities. The actions and comments may spring from stereotypes, prejudices, or biases. The microaggressor may or may not realize the actions or words are invalidating or even that they are expressing negative thoughts (sometimes they think they are being complimentary), but that does not make the comment any less egregious. The harm in the microaggressive comment exceeds the offense caused by ill manners or poor taste. Microaggression is cumulatively felt and can swiftly, incisively revisit trauma on the person experiencing it.

Below are examples of microaggressions that are experienced by various groups or individuals, how they are received, and what that ultimately communicates to the hearer or receiver.

Spoken or Demonstrated Microaggression	What Is Heard by Those to Whom the Remark/ Behavior Is Directed	Extended Meaning (impact even though intent might be different)
What are you? Where are you from?	You must not be from around here because of the way you look. This is exoticizing and othering.	Only white people are truly American. If you don't look white, you belong to another, inferior team. You are expected to know and declare your family history at the request of a white person.
I'm colorblind. I don't see color. I don't see you as any different than I am.	Being nonwhite is problematic, but somehow you are the exception. As a person of color, you can expect to be mistreated or ignored and erased and your heritage discounted, so be happy that I see you as "normal."	White people get to make the determination about whether you are worthy or not.

Spoken or Demonstrated Microaggression	What Is Heard by Those to Whom the Remark/ Behavior Is Directed	Extended Meaning (impact even though intent might be different)
You're gay? You don't look gay!	There's a certain discernible way to look as a gay person, and you haven't measured up. The less gay you look, the more acceptable you are to society.	Being gay or straight has a right or wrong to it, and you are being judged.
Can I touch your hair? Someone reaches out and without permission touches, pats, pulls, or scrunches the hair of a person of color.	Your (Black, curly, coily, kinky) hair is so exotic and othered that you are a curiosity, almost pet-like.	You are very different and must be so different from a white person that it's understandable why you should not be integrated. As a white person, I am allowed to break boundaries of personal space whenever I wish for any reason. There's a legacy of this behavior that recalls slave markets where the grade and type of hair were examined by the white person's hand during the selling process.
Wow! You're so articulate!	It's surprising that a Brown or Black person like you can enunciate clearly or speak intelligently.	Nonwhite people and particularly Black and Brown people are far inferior to white people and cannot be counted on to speak comprehensibly about anything significant.

(continued)

When Beliefs and Actions Collide

Spoken or Demonstrated Microaggression	What Is Heard by Those to Whom the Remark/ Behavior Is Directed	Extended Meaning (impact even though intent might be different)
Are you a man or woman?	I'm uncomfortable with the idea that I can't place you and determine for myself what I want to call you or how to imagine you.	There's a binary to which you should belong, and if you can't tell me you are one or another in terms of gender, I will think less of you. You are trying to trick or fool me by how you present yourself.
Are you pregnant? When are you due? Congratulations!	You are gaining weight; you look different, and I want to call it out to others; you are a sexual being and I'm uncomfortable about that, so I'll be overly effusive in my observations and how I react.	Anyone can or should judge or comment on a woman's body and make assumptions about her fertility.
You're Asian, right? You must be in the IT department. Will you help me fix my computer?	As a person of color who is Asian, I am immediately thought to be proficient in math and science. This is not necessarily complimentary: I do not want to be reduced to a skill set even if it's an admirable one.	I will first be looked at two-dimensionally as a worker, then as a person.
You're not handicapped. You're handicapable!	You are superhuman because "something is wrong with you" and you still show up in public. You would probably be mediocre or inferior if you didn't have a disability.	People with disabilities make me uncomfortable, and I'm surprised to see them living life. Shouldn't they all be unhappy and failing instead of trying to thrive?

A REMINDER: THE WHAT OF DEAI

We must be careful about the way we treat each other and how we interact inside the museum as well as outside. We must also, above all, be caring. A DEAI platform is not a way to attract and hire more employees, market to new audiences, befriend the local community, or curry favor with foundations and funders even if these are outcomes. Pointing out the better and kinder ways to describe and relate to others is only a way to reduce suffering for all concerned. We should learn to take gentle correction and patient instruction gracefully.

A DEAI platform is our authentic contribution to the peaceful world we seek as we grapple with an inequitable, still-oppressive world. It's a collective effort by all museum constituents, so we will learn and grow together in service of that goal. While everyone is welcome to the museum and we all matter as leaders, employees, visitors, and would-be visitors, ultimately, the DEAI focus is for those with the least power, privilege, and access. It's about acknowledging and redressing the harms of people who have been or are still being unjustly neglected, unfairly treated, willfully minoritized, and historically hidden from museums. This group is larger than you might think and includes far more than racial, ethnic, gender-based, and sexual orientation minorities. It also includes socioeconomic status especially where the status has been chronic and generational. It includes those with visible and hidden disabilities. Some of you might be privileged in some ways and lack significant power in other ways. The principles and practices of DEAI should engender compassion and help museum practitioners seek justice with empathy.

Another strategy that assists in this aim is to intentionally create figurative and literal zones of safety in the museum's workspaces. Here, staff can share origin stories, do the work of cultural competency, practice emotional intelligence skills, and begin to problem-solve—not as part of exhibition development or program planning but to better understand and support each other. These internal inclusion zones might be a dedicated office space or the corner of a lunchroom; it might be where the DEAI offices are located; it might be a different spot each month; it might be at a favorite community café. Museum staff, board members, leaders, and volunteers should be regularly reminded that it's not only acceptable to encourage productive discussions about diversity, justice, and inclusion, but it's an expectation.

Personal journal entries can pique interest and drum up relevant questions. Staff members and others may wish to gather together to write and sketch in their journals privately while together. As museum practitioners continue to write in their journals and consume thoughtful information, they may wish to speak with others about what they are learning and how it applies to their daily DEAI challenges. These questions should be taken to the internal public square to become stimulating dialogue that ameliorates behavior happening in the museum and in the communities the museum serves. Practicing ways to talk about inclusion can ensure that correct terms are used and that there is ease and facility in dialogue. Hopefully, there will be a mix of organic informal conversations occurring as well as formal professional development opportunities as an outgrowth.

Activities that might be conducted in these casual meetings might be about interrupting microaggressions, overcoming the fear of DEAI work, practicing how to speak respectfully to each other, and practicing conversations with people who hold more or less privilege and power as a museum family.

Try not to let these meetings devolve into gossip sessions about individuals or negative talk about your bosses. You may wish to practice calling in while calling out if you find the sessions are becoming destructive rather than constructive. If you are talking about how to help those with organizational power delegate responsibilities in an equitable way and someone in the group starts naming an unkind supervisor or specific situation known to all in the meeting, try to gently call that person or behavior in without shaming or scolding. You may want to remind the entire group of the task at hand as in "We only have a few minutes before the museum opens to the public. Let's stick to the general topic, and let's also remember this is a team-building exercise and so-and-so is part of the team."

SENSE OF HUMOR

Having a sense of humor is highly important when you are building and deepening relationships. Managing conflict is partially about respecting the values that are sacred to others, including how you consider things that can be laughed at and those that should be kept off-limits.

As a general rule, laughter at the expense of others is unacceptable. Occasional self-deprecation is OK as is sarcasm directed at people with privilege unconnected to our daily lives. Cutting remarks about people with whom you engage on a daily basis and with whom you are trying to build relationships is never, ever a good idea.

A sense of humor can help you connect with others, look past their flaws, and relieve tension together in an uplifting, joyous way. Laughter is good medicine. The best jokes to enjoy as a museum group are ones that are lighthearted, fun, and inclusive. Finding little juxtapositions in everyday observations, using clean wordplay and puns, and giggling at the absurdities of life can be a delight.

Your diversity, equity, accessibility, and inclusion approach is also about being more sentient, caring, emotionally intelligent people. Those who are emotionally intelligent understand that there is more than one way of doing things and of being right about things. Emotional intelligence is about being aware and understanding of our own and others' emotions so we can navigate and influence them successfully to reach our goals.

The word *conflict* has two major definitions. There is the long, protracted battle either of the soul or an actual combat of troops. Then, there are minor conflicts—tensions, abrasions, and touch points that spark and fizzle just as quickly. Conflict is not always bad. Sometimes it can be welcomed. Even the wrestlings of the spirit tend to fortify and strengthen the person who overcomes. Sometimes simple misunderstandings between two entities are quickly resolvable and have no negative intent.

The vowel sounds in the Spanish language are open and consistent, relying on only a handful of varying intonations marked by straightforward accent signs. Written word for word, Spanish and Portuguese look rather similar but for a wider variety of accent marks in Portuguese on both vowels and consonants. Portuguese has dozens of vowel inflections, and some are not easily discernible by an untutored ear. A simple three-letter word that a one-year-old can say is easily understood and pronounced by native Portuguese speakers but a non-Portuguese speaker might struggle for months or more to make sure they lift their palate to the needed height and direct airflow to the right section of the nasal cavity for the correct duration of time as they pronounce the monosyllabic word for "dad" without saying "bread" instead. In Spanish, words that looked almost identical would sound almost identical, but in Portuguese, the auditory differences are far subtler. Patience, kindness, humor, and assuming the best, rather than the worst, intentions of others are essential in bridging gaps in communication between or among different groups.

When you consider that to the day-to-day interactions of people from the same museum culture and the same geographic culture who work together are sometimes already in conflict, it is little wonder that a new institutional push for changing the composition of the workforce, reallocating resources and amending some of its policies and structures in favor of those who typically do not benefit, welcoming audiences who historically were not expected or invited to make use of the museum's offerings, and demanding better interactions internally is going to cause even more friction. Let's look at these individually.

COMMUNITIES IN CRISIS (CONTEXTUAL)

- LGBTQIA+
- Employees over forty
- People with disabilities
- People with economic need
- BIPOC
- Jewish people
- Blacks
- Women
- Asians
- Those who identify as Islamic or Muslim
- New immigrants
- Refugees

- People who don't use English as their first language
- Others

Which ones of these communities do you believe to be most in crisis nationally and in what ways?

Which of these communities are most in crisis in your immediate vicinity and in what ways?

If you don't know the answers to the above questions, how can you find out as a group?

For those who don't believe that any or many of these groups are in some way marginalized by society, community, and museums, what examples can you give to them?

Your examples might include those of potential physical, emotional, or psychological harm, microaggressions, or prejudiced behavior.

Are there members of these groups in your museums who are

- board members,
- leadership team members,
- staff members, or
- volunteers or interns?

Have you ever thought that they too might need support? What can you do to empathetically listen to and accept them for their authentic selves, help them feel more secure at the museum, and be a friend and ally where warranted?

Do they have organizational power, or do they not have any decision-making power in the museum? If there are members of these groups in your activity, allow them to speak up and speak for themselves. Let them tell their stories in the absence of fear, judgment, or repercussion. Note that some people from marginalized identities or cultural communities may not consider themselves to be without power or privilege.

ACTIVITY 1

Embarrassing Moment Sharing Circle and Reflection (20 minutes)
Objectives: Team Building, Practicing Personal Storytelling with Humor

- Form a circle and gather up to eight people in each group.
- Hand each person in the group a sticky note and a marker.
- Ask everyone in the group to think of a (safe for work) embarrassing moment they would like to share.
- Have each person write on the sticky note an appropriate title for their story, such as "Signed a work email with 'love'" or "Wore two different shoes."
- Let each person stick their story title on a whiteboard or wall.

- One by one, call participants up to read a title and have the corresponding storyteller recount the whole story. Everyone should listen intently (and laugh appropriately!) until the story is completed.
- After everyone has had a turn, conduct a five-minute reflection about the value of vulnerability, the importance of being able to laugh at oneself, and the fact that we all have embarrassing things happen to us. See if there are any similar stories.
- Pledge to support each other despite the humor we find in situations beyond our control that can be funny.

OUTWARD EXERCISES

TESTING OUR TERMS

Have you ever used the terms *at-risk, minorities, underserved, underrepresented,* or *in need*? To whom exactly are you referring? Use the form below to write four sentences about why you might be using these terms. An example below uses the term *minorities*.

Note: We are not talking about or arguing against using euphemisms. This exercise is about focusing on the terms we are using to acknowledge the people behind the terms. Sometimes our choices can reveal biases that can become microaggressions—even if these terms are institutionalized as terms of the trade. Think about why and how you use these terms, if there are better word choices you could make, and whether you and your colleagues can challenge others with whom you work outside of the museum to use more inclusive phrases.

Term	*Who This Term Describes*	*Why I Have Used This Term*	*A More Precise Term to Use*
Minorities	1. BIPOC, Indigenous/Native Americans, Latinx people, immigrants (especially those who do not speak English or who are nonwhite)	I see it written everywhere. It's the term I hear on TV and in the media. It's what I grew up using.	People who have been marginalized by society, museums, America, the world

6

Clashing Cultures

CULTURE: THE WAY WE DO THINGS AROUND HERE

We all come from somewhere. Our home groups, with their elders, parent figures, mentors, and peers, shape our beliefs and teach us by word and deed how to behave in ways that are acceptable and laudatory. Acting contrary to the norms sometimes brings physical or psychological expulsion.

When some think of culture, they think of the arts and heritage of people far away who bear characteristics far different than the ones we hold. They see handcrafted objects, batiked fabrics, painted skulls, or dances that are done by adults and children from a certain geographic area, and they say, "Cool! That's culture." They don't realize that culture might also be sitting down on a cold aluminum bench to watch a football game for hours on a weekend; or sitting together in church on Sunday; or waving cheerfully at yet another Spock, saying, "Live long and prosper! I'll see you at the next convention!"; or any number of collective behaviors and expectations that set us apart and make us who we are.

Culture is simply the way things are done where we are. What's acceptable? What's not? Where are the boundaries? Do we belong? We all belong to more than one culture and have various identities, some of which are also cultural. You may want to explore the differences between identity and culture in your journals. Which identities are also cultures? Do you reject an identity that is part of a general culture but still feel part of a culture? For instance, do you identify with a certain religion but eschew the teachings and values of that religion or have been excommunicated from it? Do you have an identity that others insist is a culture but you believe is not?

Some cultures gain and retain strength due to their historical heft even when struggle and pain are the undercurrents. This does not make any of their struggle delightful or deserved. The pain they carry may be part of their culture and should be honored as it is expressed in their storytelling, sacred dance and prayer, need for their own land and nations, or reparations and their languages, accents, and dialects. Cultures of Native American peoples across the Western Hemisphere—from Canada to the United States to the Caribbean and Central America and South America—were ill-treated, many nearly or completely destroyed, all colonized, all terrorized, most Christianized by force. People abducted from Africa and unwillingly scattered across the North and South American continents share similar histories but over the hundreds of years since, have developed different cultural practices and variances in cultural traits, but the similarities are striking. Even within these cultures, some set themselves apart as racially, ethnically, or regionally different. For example, Latinx people in the West Indies who are of African descent might acknowledge their African lineage while those in the Gulf of Mexico might not.

Certainly, there are groups we realize as cultural today that are bonded due to religious beliefs, or geographic connectedness, or other reasons besides violence and trauma bonding. Any group that shares similar traits, values, practices, and alignments can be a cultural group. Groups that practice and continue the artistic fruits of their shared or others' cultural activities could also be a culture. Youth culture, aging culture, techie culture, Deaf culture—these are cultures too. Some need to be paid more attention to than others in a museum context whether it's because they have historically been marginalized or misunderstood, they are underrepresented in museums, or for some other reason.

MUSEUMS AND MATERIAL CULTURE

In a guest lecture to a class of museum studies students once, I posed the question: "What are the similarities and differences between a museum and an amusement park?" The responses were curious—some were hilarious, some poignant, and some were illuminating. The answers gave great insight to the reason so many vibrant young people with such varied interests are equally interested in museums as a career.

Museums are about people and material culture. Museums exist to display, study, preserve, and honor objects that hold aesthetic, cultural, scientific, and historical significance. They also exist to delight, create a sense of wonder, educate, and enthrall. For these tasks, a highly skilled staff with a variety of specialized bases of knowledge is required. In one of my favorite museums, I worked with people who in former careers were seamstresses, schoolteachers, army and navy officers, priests, anthropologists, carpenters, artists, and electricians. Some of them had additional museology education, and some did not. We understood museum culture and took unique advantage of our synergy. We shared several cultural similarities beyond our museum culture. We all lived in the same area, had resided there for years, and shared the same cultural beliefs. When there was a need to write a label or create a facsimile connected to our museum artifacts, we were all of a shared understanding of what that would entail. As the lone nonwhite person on staff, I frequently had to code-switch or cover to fit in more seamlessly, but I still belonged to the religious culture and, thereby, relied on that aspect of my cultural makeup to fit in and work easily within the creative environment.

Moving out East and working with people from a variety of racial, ethnic, generational, religious, and other cultures provided interesting experiences—exhilarating, even—but it was sometimes harder to understand my colleagues and there was more disagreement among us. I had been raised to consider discord a bad thing, so I was very puzzled and spent inordinate amounts of time trying to agree instead of enjoying and understanding the different viewpoints for what they were. The exhibitions I worked on and the education programming I helped to develop were somehow more layered and thought provoking than anything I'd collaboratively worked on at the previous ones. Many years later as I muse on this, I am convinced that by engaging with people from various racial, ethnic, national origins; people across the LGBTQIA+ spectrum; even those who were from other religions—and even atheists!—listening keenly to what they had to say and trying to see through their own cultural lenses as invited, I became a better professional, friend, and person. Later, I was even able to successfully navigate a faith transition and be truer to myself in ways I could never have imagined before.

Working with people from other cultural realms is exciting, but it's also hard. It does take time, patience, and energy and is difficult in the same way learning a new language is—especially if that language is you adjacent. We expect that people should be "just like us" and even prefer it as an oft-used bias. Affinity bias seeks those who are similar in terms of identity and culture and tells us they merit the seal of approval because they are like us and can be trusted.

Cultural clashes in museums are amplified when we don't know enough about ourselves and each other. These clashes take the form of petty disagreements stemming from bias and privilege; differences of opinion on technical judgments; differences in cultural values, perspectives, and expectations; and differences between and among museum employees, visitors, and communities. Here are some common cultural clashes and strategies for working through them as they come up in museums by department or work area.

REPRESENTATION AND INTERPRETATION (CURATION, EXHIBITIONS, AND EDUCATION)

Cultural Clash: Disagreements may arise when staff, volunteers, and community experts are choosing how to represent and interpret the artifacts and stories of certain cultures or sensitive historical events especially if there are differing perspectives or potential controversies and where there are members of those cultures represented. The absence of individuals from the cultures being represented would be highly problematic. Staff members who might be invited to participate in the planning process may be invited by virtue of their supposed ethnic or racial background, but they may not actually practice or share the cultural mores of the art's creator. Cultural groups are not monoliths whether through time or space.

Solutions: Encourage open dialogue and collaboration among museum employees and with visitors and community members. Seek input from people from diverse races, ethnicities, national origins, and other cultures, engaging in respectful discussions to ensure multiple views are considered. Implement inclusive interpretation strategies that reflect culturally responsive input and patiently engage in critical dialogue. Make no assumptions about the contributors' backgrounds and personal stories.

OWNERSHIP AND REPATRIATION

Cultural Clash: Museums may be in possession of artifacts or cultural objects that are considered sacred or of significant cultural importance to certain communities. Disputes may arise regarding ownership and provenance. As museum practitioners seeking to reduce harm to each other, our admiring public, and visitors we have yet to meet, we must be transparent and humble in handling these matters. Land acknowledgments are only helpful if they are accompanied by empathy, conversation, and action.

Solutions: Establish clear policies and procedures for addressing repatriation requests. Engage in respectful dialogue with community representatives to understand their perspectives and concerns. Consider repatriation options, such as long-term loans or collaborative exhibitions, that respect cultural ownership while still allowing for public access and education. Note that these options should not be sought if they are highly sacred or fragile.

ACCESSIBILITY AND INCLUSION

Cultural Clash: Museums may face challenges in prioritizing accessibility and inclusion strategies for a multiplicity of diverse audiences, including those with disabilities, different cultural backgrounds, and whose first language is not English, in the face of limited resources. Since a large number of people have a defined disability, including hidden disabilities, almost everyone is affected, and people deal with their own and their loved ones' disabilities in different ways. After an informative museum daylong workshop, a director of operations confronted the presenter, angrily disagreeing about her suggestion to use inclusive person-first language for people with disabilities. "My sister doesn't mind that I call her a crip! She likes it! She enjoys having us carry her around!" It was shocking to hear, but a good lesson that even people from the cultures who can be supported by the best principles and practices of accessibility may have other personal or cultural reasons for disagreeing.

Solutions: Conduct regular accessibility audits to identify barriers and make necessary improvements, considering those with accommodation needs and requests primarily. Use principles of universal design, recognizing that thoughtfully implemented solutions can help resolve multiple issues. Your DEAI office should include a position entirely dedicated to accessibilities for people with disabilities and for disability justice. Engage with community organizations and individuals to understand their needs and collaborate on inclusive programming and exhibitions. Provide training for museum staff on cultural sensitivity and accessible practices.

STAFF DIVERSITY AND REPRESENTATION

Cultural Clash: Lack of representation among museum staff can lead to cultural clashes and misunderstandings when engaging with communities of color, various ethnic communities, LGBTQIA+ communities, and others.

Solution: Actively promote diversity and inclusion in hiring practices to ensure a range of perspectives and experiences within the museum staff. Provide cultural competency training to employees to enhance their understanding of different cultures and foster respectful interactions. Encourage ongoing dialogue and learning opportunities to address any cultural clashes that may arise. You may want to adopt a sibling museum that is doing well in this area and is willing to communicate with your teams on an idea-sharing, friend-raising basis.

FUNDING AND PRIORITIES

Cultural Clash: Differences in funding priorities and expectations between museum administrators and community stakeholders can lead to conflicts regarding resource allocation and programming decisions. Museum norms and biases that dictate certain kinds of behaviors, such as outreach programs, can stigmatize and marginalize people living and attending schools in certain areas; museums refusing to make concessions for people according to their needs may be accepted by some board and staff members and not by others.

Solution: Foster transparent communication between museum administrators and community stakeholders to understand their respective priorities and limitations. Seek opportunities for collaboration and shared decision-making to align funding priorities with community needs. Engage in ongoing dialogue to address any conflicts and find mutually beneficial solutions.

Addressing cultural clashes in museums requires open communication, collaboration, and a commitment to inclusivity and respect. By actively engaging with communities, seeking diverse perspectives, and implementing inclusive practices, museums can work through misunderstandings and disappointments between cultures (including museum culture) and foster positive relationships with their staff and the communities they serve.

ASSESSING YOUR MUSEUM'S CULTURAL COMPETENCE

Measuring and understanding your level of cultural competence can be a helpful strategy on your journey to greater acceptance of other ways of doing and being. Members of your team may need help in understanding why intercultural competence is essential to communicating effectively and how it can be germane to achieving justice.

Several cultural competence tools exist, one of which is the Intercultural Development Inventory, or IDI. The IDI is a widely used instrument that measures an individual's or organization's capacity to shift cultural perspective. It assesses the complexity with which people experience cultural difference and similarity, and unlike other instruments that factor in personal traits or characteristics, looks at how an individual might adapt behavior when presented with a shift in cultural perspective. The IDI is based on Dr. Milton Bennett's Developmental Model of Intercultural Sensitivity (DMIS).

7

Don't We All Matter?

WHY TOLERANCE AND KINDNESS ARE NOT ENOUGH

I need to say a word here about niceness. Museum people can be the most pleasant of folks when it comes to hospitality and transactional communication. Like many museum practitioners, other places of employment I have worked included service industries that relied on the short-term satisfaction of the consumers. In my case, as a teen or young woman, I had short-term stints as a hotel housekeeper, shop attendant, elevator girl, and information desk worker. Each of these jobs required being polite, servile, or even obsequious.

When it comes to working with the public, museum staff are known for smiles and bending over backward to appease, entertain, and mollify. This kind of fawning politeness is understandable and acceptable from a transactional standpoint. Exhibits and galleries are not long-form experiences, however, and responsive staff who are looking out for our guests and each other should be trained in how to deescalate unwanted behavior; identify and interrupt microaggressions; and work with medical teams, law enforcement, and others. This is not solely the province of guest services. Labels we create may have viewpoints on them that are disagreeable to some people. Visitors should be informed of rules that prohibit them from wearing clothing or engaging in on-site behaviors that are upsetting, abusive, or threatening to other visitors and staff. An organization that stands for justice has to make difficult decisions and take its stand boldly and bravely. We cannot be all things to all people, conciliatory to every opinion and behavior of visitors or community members when that behavior means it is physically, psychologically, or emotionally harmful to others.

Tolerating viewpoints that further oppress and mock the principles of justice that you are trying to uphold is wrong. How do we discern what is intolerable? It is important to remember that we see things from our own points of view far more often than we do through others'. When we say we see everyone as equals or treat everyone equally, we might actually be demonstrating that we are only valuing people for their sameness and not paying attention to their individual differences.

Tolerance in itself is not a bad thing nor is trying to be nice and treating people well. The trouble with tolerance is there is a shallowness to it that doesn't allow us to appreciate the meaningful nuances that humanize each of us. We can encounter a vexing, complex situation that challenges our biases or opinions. When faced with new knowledge, we might be moved to change our mentality just enough to say we tolerate the new insight or the person we don't quite understand. Tolerating has an inherent hesitancy about it. Tolerance is just a threshold and not the full entrance into the room.

Must we treat each other with dignity and respect? When it comes to people who would denigrate, harm, and belittle us because of racist beliefs or some other bigoted or hateful ideal, we can tolerate or respect their right to have an opinion, but we do not and should not have to countenance their threatening behavior; nor do we have to tolerate them. We can show people the museum door. We can have a compact of respectful behavior to which we hold our visitors, staff, and our other publics. We can enforce rules about not wearing hateful slogans on our clothes in the buildings and anywhere we sponsor programs and event. We can mandate the expectations we need to have to ensure the safety of others and especially those who have been unsafe by neglect or design.

During a DEAI workshop one day, I mentioned that anti-racism wasn't enough but that we should be pro–People of Color too. There was silence in this room of about forty, with three People of Color also in the room, including me. After a small beat, a woman raised her hand timidly and asked, "Do we have to?" I quickly answered, "Yes!"

I don't know how the other Black people in the room felt that day, but I felt a sad combination of embarrassment, discomfort, being unsafe, and annoyance. Was it that heavy a lift, that great a burden to be cheerfully on the side of someone who was not like them? Just how strange or unpalatable did they find BIPOC individuals? Are we that unlikeable? What is it about being pro, or for, people who are from another ethnic background that seems unfathomable or unpalatable?

If we don't take time to learn and love other cultures; the products of those cultures; and the people who create, live, and operate within those values, we are apt to allow bias to fill in the gaps and create alternate stories for us. We might not enjoy each and every artistic product, or foodstuff, or manner of speech or presentation, but we can appreciate and try to understand with positivity and grace—and dare I say, enthusiasm.

Kindness and smiles might be genuine, or they might mask the contempt of antagonistic people. Shakespeare described how "one can smile, and smile, and be a villain." I have worked with people in museums who radiated acceptance, goodness, and authenticity. I have worked with others who smiled in public to hide their truly specious natures and in private, with individuals they disdain or despise in ways that are cruel and cutting. Disingenuity is antithetical to the openness and vulnerability that should pervade in a DEAI approach.

We can practice going beyond tolerance in interpersonal ways, interacting with each other in ways that promote respect, open-mindedness, and inclusivity.

There is much that we can learn from science museums and children's museums. The contemporary science museum, as differentiated from the 19th-century natural history museum, is largely a place for equitable exploration. Children's museums are also known for providing a wide range of hands-on educational experiences that are meant to be enjoyable and inclusive. These kinds of museums must also dig deep to see what else they are missing. They must still look inwardly as individual practitioners to root out bias, collaborate as colleagues to determine how not to let bias infect their practice, identify systemic challenges in their organizations, and course correct with humility and justice when necessary. I've heard some children's museum workers say that issues surrounding DEAI are too adult for children or simply not relevant. Once again, the question must be: Not relevant for whom? The child who is not seeing inventors or scientists who look like them might disagree. When gender minorities and sexual orientation minorities are not observed or included or when opportunities for visitor dialogue are not explored, there may be more they, too, can do. Teaching tolerance is not enough.

Another way that we can use our tolerance to uphold anti-oppressive ideals is to practice ethical behavior in work groups and committees.

Ethics committees can be very effective in helping to shape both brave and safe spaces. Led by the DEAI committee, select board members, leadership team members, or staff across the organization, museums should hold regular ethics meetings to educate themselves on critical issues in museum ethics both broadly and specifically regarding your institution's challenges. Topics of concern might include the following:

- Identifying the fundamental civil and human rights that your museum will publicly and consistently foster, uphold, and protect.
- Creating new policies for employees based on the principles of ethics and justice.
- Engaging in ongoing sensitivity and anti-oppression training.
- Encouraging staff to continue personal journaling and interstaff communication about inclusion and anti-oppression.

- Positioning the museum as a place of safety from oppression and harm
- Aligning with Codes of Ethics from the International Council on Museums (ICOM), American Alliance of Museums (AAM), American Association for State and Local History (AASLH), Association of Science Technology Centers (ASTC), Association of Children's Museums (ACM), and other governing bodies of national and international museum significance.
- Engaging with and preparing to interact with your surrounding communities, particularly those who question your sincerity, capacity, motives, and authenticity.
- Continuing to learn and grow together without becoming jaded.

GROUP EXERCISE: I HEAR YOU

Are we listening respectfully, or are we just waiting for the noise to stop?

An excellent way to practice keen listening is to gather in pairs or small groups with coworkers and engage in team-building exercises geared to improving trust and emotional safety.

In small groups of two to four, take turns around a circle taking the role of either a speaker or listener. Set a timer for two and a half minutes and listen to the speaker give a brief talk about something meaningful to them, such as their family of origin, their pet, their experiences as someone who is marginalized or someone from a dominant culture group. During the talk, the listeners should only listen, not fidget, not try to jump in with questions, and not zone out. After the first speaker has had a turn, leave one minute for questions. Very likely, that will not be enough time for questions. Even so, continue with the exercise until everyone has had a turn. Afterward, write in your individual journal. What was the exercise like? Did you find yourself wanting to join in? Do you feel uncomfortable if you are not the one speaking? What did you learn about yourself and your colleagues both in terms of what they said and how they listened?

8

More than a Checklist

WHY CREATING AND CHECKING OFF A BULLETED LIST RINGS HOLLOW

In every museum, there are various key staff who are confused about or resistant to transforming the museum or even discussing the need to be a more inclusive space.

At one museum where I worked, a predictable few from the peanut gallery would moan and complain each time mandatory or strongly encouraged DEAI workshops were scheduled. "We've already done racism," one of them famously said.

Even though this attitude (spoken or unvoiced) is becoming increasingly rare, it still raises its hands, pointing to our greater need to communicate the severity of DEAI challenges at every level and job function within a museum organization and to explain that it is an iterative process that will take transparency and time to resolve.

It is certain that museum teams will face various levels of buy-in as they initiate and continue their DEAI work. Their reticence or refusal may have roots in their disbelief in or unwillingness to accept ideologies promoting justice. In other strategies to build diversity or build audiences, such behavior could be masked by a checklist approach. After all, a checklist approach is doing the bare minimum.

Some of the naysayers or more intransigent staff or board members may go through the motions but stop progress on the checklist, citing time or budget concerns.

When I'm contacted by someone such as this who wants me to send them a checklist as well as a standard list of resources to read so they can make their museums inclusive and anti-racist, I respond to them, usually spending an hour on the phone with them explaining that it's not so simple. What they're asking me for is a weekly grocery shopping list and a carton of cookbooks when they really want a piping hot meal on the table. I don't provide that kind of list because they need to do the internal work of understanding what comprises a delicious and healthy meal, how many people they're feeding, what preferences and allergies their family members or guests might have and how to accommodate them, and how to go about preparing the food from scratch by adapting recipes.

DEAI work is relational, situational, and contextual. The situations that arise with one group of museum leaders and staff will be different challenges that happen under another leader's watch. Staff and priorities change and leaders leave. Lists are low-priority items.

To extend the analogy, my naming the best greengrocers at which to shop or defining trends in gastronomy have very little to do with the actual day-to-day work of understanding the chemical processes of baking and parboiling; the rudiments of binding a sauce; the inexpensive but equally nutrient-rich substitutions for certain fats, proteins, and carbohydrates; or the tastes of their own families and guests.

Cooking nutritious meals and eating regularly around a table can change a culture and create community. Obtaining names of grocery stores or brands of food items will not go far enough in creating change and can ultimately add to confusion, becoming an impediment to or excuse for inaction.

Meanwhile, people grow or remain hungry.

Checklists work only in the initial brainstorming stage, which has to be done by museum staff who deeply understand their own museum culture and the individuals who will be implementing the rigors of the DEAI program. An assessment of the museum practitioners' cultural capacity is always helpful, as it may divulge hidden and perhaps unknown impediments to thoroughly understanding the heavy intercultural lift at hand.

Insisting on checklists or believing that the DEAI initiative is a brief time-based element within a much larger strategy for the museum is to miscalculate the complexity and nuance involved in anti-oppression work. Checklists focus on surface-level activities rather than delving into the underlying system issues that must be addressed.

If the diversity, equity, accessibility, and inclusion efforts do not combine to yield restorative justice, what you have or want is a set of activities and not an anti-oppression societal framework for change.

Diversity and inclusion work cannot simply entail ticking off boxes or meeting quotas. It requires a profound understanding of the historical and social contexts that led and continue to lead to exclusion and marginalization. Checklists often fail to capture the complexity of these issues and may lead to superficial efforts that do not result in the kind of change that is transformative.

Checklists can also breed complacency and a false sense of accomplishment. When organizations rely solely on checklists, they may believe that by completing the tasks on the list, they have achieved their diversity and inclusion goals. However, diversity and inclusion are ongoing processes that require continual evaluation, reflection, and adaptation. Checklists can give the illusion of progress without actually addressing the underlying biases and structural barriers that perpetuate exclusion.

Furthermore, checklists may not adequately capture the diverse experiences and perspectives of different identities, cultural groups, and communities. DEAI requires a deep understanding of the specific needs and challenges faced by relevant marginalized groups.

Checklists fail to capture the nuances and complexities of these experiences, leading to generic and ineffective strategies. A one-size-fits-all approach does not account for the unique histories, cultures, and identities of different communities. They can inadvertently reinforce tokenism and performative actions. When organizations focus solely on checking off diversity-related tasks, they may prioritize quantity over quality. This can lead to tokenistic gestures that do not result in meaningful change or create an inclusive environment. True diversity and inclusion require a commitment to creating equitable systems and addressing power imbalances, which makes imperative time, patience, intellect, and ability to achieve.

Checklists can be useful for organizing tasks and ensuring that certain steps are taken; there are many such brainstorming prompts throughout this book. Note that they are not to be confused with actual and often strategic diversity and inclusion planning. Diversity and inclusion work that leads to justice-forward initiatives requires a deep understanding of complex issues; ongoing evaluation and reflection; and a commitment on the part of all participants to recognize, address, and acknowledge systemic barriers.

9

Respectful Dialogue and Conversations That Lead to Lasting Change

This chapter begins with the assumption that, currently, your museum family does not speak to each other at all outside of requisite meetings. In some museums, staff members rush around with heads down, nary a friendly greeting or nod to their fellow employees. It can be absolutely withering and demoralizing.

On the other hand, museums whose staff actually enjoy each other's company are delightful. I've worked at a few museums where smiles and even embraces are regular greetings and affection is unfeigned. Just recently I spoke to three former colleagues of more than twenty years ago, all of whom have kept in touch over time. When museum colleagues begin with respect for themselves and each other, the ground is ripe for teaching and learning about culture, compassion, and community.

A former museum gallery attendant posted a review of their work experience on a notorious social media platform, giving a popular regional museum only two stars: The only pro was "lunch break," and the numerous cons included "Unpaid lunch, have to stand all shift, can't talk to coworkers, low pay, mind-numbing, can't have water on job." It's almost insulting to expect full immersion into an anti-oppression initiative when the museum is itself oppressive to its own staff members. There's always room to grow, however, and it takes a while to change a culture.

The first step is simply to trust, to expect trust, to give trust, to be trustworthy. With trust in the process and the people, a pact can be formed among the constituents. With trust comes respect, and respectful language follows.

We want to maintain that trust so we can connect with vulnerability and kindness. Trust implies honesty among partners and a desire to think the best of them and believe them at their word.

The first principle of respectful dialogue is to take people at their word. If parties are poised to mean what they say and say what they mean, they are ready to be accountable to each other and themselves. Dialogue implies equal, open participation of all involved.

Will everyone in your museum agree to the DEAI approach you have chosen, the activities you use, and the principles you espouse? No, they won't. We can guarantee that will be the case. Thankfully, when people are pleasant, kind, and trusting, they will work in accordance with the plan to facilitate the cause. Questioning and disagreeing can be done respectfully, affirming each other's dignity and worth. Interrogating the process need not be destructive or mean; when colleagues are truly working for the good of the order, inquisitive discourse need not get personal.

Interaction does not have to be formal to be inclusive. In fact, insisting on formal communication might actually be imposing a dominant culture imperative on other cultures needlessly and to their detriment. Respectful dialogue and using inclusive language come from being culturally responsive, or being attentive to the cultural practices of those with whom you are in conversation, and engaging at the cultural level that is most comfortable, natural, and efficient for them. Like the example of Spanish or Portuguese versus Portunhol, strive for Portunhol. Examples of this kind of respectful, inclusive expectation might be disregarding a different national or regional accent as an unspoken qualification for hiring or realizing that so-called broken English or pidgin might just be the kind of English or other language a colleague speaks and writes—we should not judge their intelligence, their ability to comprehend, or their worth as an individual based on these traits. Respectful dialogue requires keen listening and caring. Altruism is a virtue to which we can subscribe.

Meeting in the middle to be more culturally responsive might even mean fewer in-person meetings and alternate or hybrid ways to communicate if people who are being asked to appear in person are being overworked and underpaid. It might mean providing food or at very least, coffee and water at certain meetings to support those who are not well compensated and are expected to work long hours with extra responsibilities.

Preparing the environment in favor of the person or people who are likely to be more vulnerable in an interaction is part of the anti-oppressive DEAI way. A helpful exercise is to always ask, "Who is most likely to be harmed in this scenario?" Harmed in this context might mean anything from embarrassed, shamed, or made to feel out of place to further marginalized or unfairly stereotyped. With thoughtful planning, there are no unhappy accidents. After all, as the multi-attributed saying goes, "Every system is perfectly designed to get the results it gets."

A much-maligned chief executive officer of a large museum was chagrined when her new open-door policy was rebuffed in short order. It didn't take long for trusting employees with the most to risk to bravely schedule visits only to feel overwhelmed by the vast, sumptuously appointed office and a leader who seemed more interested in showing it off than in listening empathetically to concerns. Any negative feedback given by an employee was taken as an insult, and every complaint was met with a challenge to quit and make way for someone else to earn minimum wage. Even though the CEO often made noise about remembering to use pronouns and the museum's vague commitment to "social inclusion," the bright demarcations of the distinct social class structure of the museum were never more evident.

Inclusive language communicates environmentally and verbally that you care about the people with whom you are interacting and are willing to do what it takes to ensure they are safe, accepted, and respected.

The use of verbiage that is culturally appropriate and bias free is essential in museum settings. Being skilled in inclusive language requires cultural awareness and a desire to transfer what you are learning about anti-oppression strategies to everyday communication. If we consider those differences that make a difference—communities and individuals that suffer continued harm as a result of colonialism, racism, gender bias, sexual orientation prejudice, religious bigotry, et cetera—we will realize how important it is to uplift them and make them visible through language. We will consider, perhaps, that by intentionally eschewing the term "mankind" for the term "humankind" we are rejecting male superiority as well as the gender binary. Most importantly, we are affirming that we are all human.

Using inclusive language is not the gotcha shell game that many people imagine. No one will get it right all the time, which is why we need to learn together in a supportive environment of trust. It's not about who knows the most about how to refer to others that's important; it's recognizing that as language develops, it can become more instructive and inclusive for clarity's sake.

HELPING EACH OTHER TO USE INCLUSIVE LANGUAGE

Gather with your colleagues in small groups to investigate and suggest the most inclusive ways to refer to people and objects in a museum context.

As a general rule for using inclusive terms, consider the following questions and whether the situation in question merits reframing your language:

1. How well do you know the individual or community you are addressing or interpreting? Remember to use the Nothing About Us Without Us principle.
2. Are you gendering a situation that doesn't call for using specifically masculine or feminine language? At times, it may be warranted, especially in cultural contexts; can you identify those and distinguish between them?

Commonly Used Word, Phrase, or Sentence in a Museum Scenario	What to Say Instead	Why
In a letter to families, your museum has written, "Mothers and fathers should pick up their children at the rotunda entrance."		
The chairman of the board is Priya Singh.		
A museum label touts "The object on view is man-made."		
A staff member timidly asks if they can use the term "Negro" to refer to Black Americans since the history exhibition is about the Negro Leagues.		
A visitor who uses a wheelchair is told "You are such an inspiration! Especially for a wheelchair person! You really inspire me! I can barely get up in the morning myself."		
The museum needs to install unisex restrooms.		
The waitress in the museum café is named Madison.		

Commonly Used Word, Phrase, or Sentence in a Museum Scenario	What to Say Instead	Why
We need more manpower on the exhibit installation team.		
The curator said, "This primitive, savage art" when referring to Polynesian artwork.		
Gather together, guys! The boss has something to say. Yes, you, too, Marjorie and Elaine!		
The director says none of us will be getting raises this year. That's so lame.		
He's just a custodian.		
You don't look disabled. Are you sure you need an accommodation?		
That candidate is too old to learn the new technology.		
Being a museum preparator is a man's job.		
Welcome to the museum, Little Man! I see you're here with your new baby sister in her frilly pink blanket! What are your names?		

3. Are you applying a gender, race, religion, nationality, or heritage to someone without actually knowing how they identify? For instance, are you saying someone is of a Hispanic ethnicity without knowing whether they speak Spanish, Portuguese, Dutch, Indigenous language, or English?
4. Do you know and understand the history and etymology behind various ways Black and Brown people identify?
5. Are you careful to avoid heteronormativity?
6. Is your speech and body language pitying or condescending toward those who have disabilities? Do you use people-first language instead of naming their condition, accommodation, or diagnosis first? Do you fawn on them for living their lives and by so doing, make them feel uncomfortable?
7. Do you make assumptions about personal relationships and associations or living situations? Do you automatically imagine that smaller children visiting the museum with adults are in a parent-and-child situation or that two adults of the same gender are siblings? Do your membership and development departments know how to address written correspondence appropriately?
8. Do you unwittingly demean people who are younger or older by your word choices?
9. Do you use language that was historically accurate and appropriate but that no longer is, for good reason?
10. Make sure that you respect the identities and cultures with which people self-identify. Use pronouns or terminology that you are asked to use without belittling, mocking, or questioning. Validate their gender and sexual identity. This refers both to people with whom you're interacting on a day-to-day basis as well as to artists and others whose work you are displaying.

10

Creating Shared Norms, Goals, Policies, and Practices

CREATING NORMS FOR RESPECTFUL CONVERSATIONS

One important practice to adopt is to verbally state norms—also called agreements—for comportment during inclusive conversations at the beginning of each planned interaction, dialogue, or meeting. I first became aware of this practice in the early 2000s when working with the Consensus Building Institute immediately after the tragedy of 9/11, while working for the John F. Kennedy Presidential Library and Museum, and again in 2007 when I headed a culturally responsive arts education program at the Pittsburgh school district. During such fraught times, workplace conversations involving multiple perspectives among people from various cultures with differing viewpoints became heated and fractious. The practice of creating shared norms of engagement helped everyone to better communicate cross culturally. Agreed-on norms describe and encourage ideal conditions under which affirmative and productive conversations would occur.

As you establish regular intervals for staff to meet and discuss DEAI ideals, when you are engaged in staff meetings and dialoguing in informal dedicated DEAI groups, make sure to read the conditions you create aloud and accept them together with some kind of outward symbol—a spoken affirmation, a thumbs-up, a firm yes, or something else. Agreeing in public is important to that shared pact.

These norms shape the atmosphere of the interaction. Think about the behavior that's most desired for full participation and the most rewarding engagement—respectful, open, vulnerable, conversational, and from the heart. Write succinct suggestions for eliciting these behaviors, such as

- keeping details confidential,
- being open-minded and open-hearted,
- allowing others to have a turn, and
- not rushing to judgment.

As you create norms that facilitate participation, vulnerability, and trust, keep in mind the notion of cultural context. When you ask your staff colleagues to be respectful, you might need to delineate what that actually means and why it's important. For someone from one culture, "respectful" might mean not speaking up at all or waiting to be called upon. For someone from another culture, interrupting a lively conversation shows a willingness to be equally participatory and excitable and is not thought of as disrespectful.

Create at least ten norms together and use them in your daily work and practice as well as during special facilitated workshops and staff meetings. These sayings can and should transcend programmatic usage.

CREATING AND DOCUMENTING SHARED GOALS (A COLLABORATIVE BRAINSTORMING PRACTICE)

As you continue working together as teams dedicated to diversity, equity, accessibility, inclusion, and anti-oppression, you will become more adept at interrogating, questioning, and wondering about the museum's goals for its DEAI approach. All members of the museum should know and understand what the museum understands to be their capacity for the work and their end goal. Does the museum want to maintain the bare standards for respectability, accreditation, or perfunctory reasons? Does the museum consider itself an organization committed to human and civil rights? Is it some of each? Can your museum constituents come to some kind of consensus as to what it can be?

Conduct surveys, convene dialogues, and confer with your strategic plans to determine what you are capable of doing and doing well. You may also wish to assess your level of cultural competence and capacity for growth to see what is possible for you at this time. You may intend to have a robust, all-encompassing program that urges staff to be champions of social justice and to focus your museum efforts on helping community members thrive, using the museum as a vehicle. It may be that your strategic plan insists that you will be the most relevant museum of your kind in the region or nation, but relevant for whom? Have you wrestled with and resolved these questions? Maybe the organizational leaders are eager to be involved in civil rights but the staff is less so. If the staff members are reticent and the museum climate is toxic, it will take much longer than you might wish or realize for your strategic goals to be realized. In that case, your museum will need to start with smaller, more achievable goals. For other museums, the majority of whose staff are eager to make changes in the world, and for those whose leadership has willingly moved from a more colonialist model to an anti-oppressive, equity-focused one, the chance of achieving at a high level is phenomenal.

A good starting document to use might be a brainstorming rubric (this is not a comprehensive checklist) to determine to what level your museum needs to focus on certain aspects of DEAI. Use this worksheet to help you. Gather as an entire staff, representational groups, or team leaders with other chosen representatives, accepting input from other staff members, to consider the following:

Diversity	Equity	Accessibility	Inclusion	Anti-oppression
Do your own work; continue with journaling.	Close pay gaps.	Budget and prepare for the expense of physical accommodations, including construction projects and improvements.	What kind of team-building activities will you conduct and commit to attending? Who on the administration and the board can commit to supporting all of these? How can you best contribute and support?	
Improve your relationships with your colleagues.	Give staff budget, time, attention, and equitable resources.			
Actively seek and hire/accept leadership of color as board members and senior staff.		Compare building code compliance with ADA and other government requirements for accessibility for buildings and grounds and make corrections where necessary.		
Create and build teams of community advisors to represent various groups and interests.				
Assess representation of marginalized groups in staff personnel.		Do a full ADA audit of buildings and grounds.		
Assess representation of marginalized groups in exhibitions and programming.				

	Diversity	Equity	Accessibility	Inclusion	Anti-oppression
Human resources	Do you have racial and ethnic diversity among the staff? What other kinds of diversity are represented?	What are ways that you can support human resources, administration, and your colleagues to recruit and hire new employees?	How can you assure incoming staff that you will be attentive to their concerns about disability accommodations as well as the visitors'? Do you affirmatively seek people with disabilities to hire?	Are you antagonistic toward or a part of the staff initiatives that promote inclusion?	
Curators/collections	Can you name and count the objects, artworks, and other elements on display that are from regions other than Europe?	Do you understand the practices and laws related to repatriation?			

Part III

Onward

11

Understanding the Relationship between Privilege and Power

MAKING DECISIONS AND KEEPING PROMISES ABOUT DEAI WORK

It's often said that the people at the head of an organization are the ones who are ultimately in charge of a company's initiatives and set the tone and example for others to follow. To a point, this is true for diversity, equity, accessibility, inclusion, and anti-oppression in a museum, with noticeable exceptions. Those with power—no matter where they are in an organization—have the most responsibility to control the DEAI work, and they know that much of that control is about letting go and ceding to those who have the least power. Power in that setting is intersectional and not always related to organizational position. It is often about who has dominant culture privilege.

There are many kinds of power besides the power held by those on the top rows of an organizational chart.

Museum leaders come from far-flung fields. Many CEOs hail from academia, private industry, federal or local government, and other trades where their skills are transferrable and their learned competencies might not translate perfectly to a museum setting. Even those who have museum credentials may find it hard to thrive as a museum leader because of museum culture, the culture of the professionals and constituents, and an ultimate lack of cultural awareness. Most of us are not trained in cultural competency. Most jobs require politeness and hospitality but not necessarily intercultural proficiency. As I like to say, museums are not widget factories, where one can punch a time clock, make widgets, check widgets, sell widgets, and repeat until retirement. Museums are about people, material culture, and relationships. To flourish in museums, one has to be adept at understanding people from a theoretical and practical standpoint while realizing that we are not all the same; we experience our lives according to our culture, and our lived experiences are filtered through the eyes of those taught either not to notice us or to notice us too much.

POWER AND ITS FUNCTIONS

A seminal study on power conducted and published in 1959 by social psychologists John R. P. French and Bertram Raven posits that there are seven (first identified as five) types of power that are accessible to individuals to motivate and direct others to achieve shared goals. When we think of power, most people envision the kind that Zeus had, hurling thunderbolts from the sky to smite his enemies. We think of the power that built empires on the backs of thousands of hapless subjects—the very power that we decry today with our anti-oppression initiatives—and we marvel at the hubris of these fearless leaders. French and Raven tell us that there are many other ways to influence others besides tactics of oppression and dominance. If we are to rid ourselves of white supremacy culture, patriarchy, prejudice, and the like in our museum workplaces and communities, it would be well to study and make use of this theory.

We all have some kind or kinds of power that we develop throughout life and bring to the museum as we begin working with others. No matter what our position, be it director or one that is considered nonessential, we may have personality traits or life skills that help us channel our abilities to lead, govern, coerce, and influence. The seven types of power follow.

- Coercive Power: Coercive power is the ability to punish or impose negative consequences on others. This kind of power relies on fear, intimidation, and the threat of punishment to influence behavior. One could imagine this power to be something that a human resources manager might need. This skill set might serve a director or CEO well, but it's not the kind that helps people feel safe in a supportive environment.
- Reward Power: Reward power is the ability to provide rewards or positive incentives to others. It involves offering benefits, recognition, promotions, or other desirable outcomes to influence behavior. Everyone likes employers who possess this kind of power or can develop and use it well. I enjoy asking museum employees to tell me about their staff meetings. Recently, a museum client told me that at their all-staff meetings, birthdays were celebrated, employee of the month awards were given, food was shared, and staff members wrote and read compliments and observations about each other. Those who initiated and maintained these kinds of practices hold reward power.
- Legitimate Power: Legitimate power comes from an individual's formal position within an organization or social structure. Those who hold

legitimate power are accepted by the group as the actual leaders who have the right to wield influence, make decisions, and hold authority. They sign the checks, speak for the museum, make the ultimate decisions, and are perceived internally and externally as the institutional leaders.

- Referent Power: This is a power that many people possess but that is often overlooked as a soft skill, yielding even softer results. To the contrary, referent power is fundamental to relationship building. It encapsulates the emotionally intelligent traits indispensable to museum DEAI work. Those with referent power greatly contribute to a positive internal culture. They are affable and easy to talk to and have the ability to construct and maintain strong relationships. The power is derived from others' admiration, respect of, and desire to be associated with that person.
- Expert Power: Expert power is derived from an individual's knowledge, skills, and expertise in a particular field or domain. Everyone who is hired, contracted, or volunteers at the museum ostensibly has expert power of some kind. Inherent in the job description and explanation of job duties is the list of skills and credentials necessary to be considered an expert in that position. Expert power is based on the perception that the person has specialized knowledge and can provide valuable insights and guidance to others. Hiring managers, department directors, and others who help build the staff in a museum do themselves a disservice if they allow bias to make personnel choices for them.
- Informational Power: Informational power is contextual, based on an individual's access to and control over valuable information. It involves having knowledge that others need or desire, which can be used to influence decisions, opinions, or actions.
- Connection Power: Connection power is based on an individual's social connections, networks, and relationships. It involves leveraging personal relationships and alliances to gain influence and access resources or opportunities. This is related to referent power but is more specific. Development and membership department members, board members, and others who fundraise and friend-raise for the museum use this power with facility and ease.

Each of these powers can be used positively or negatively, and their efficacy may vary by context and individuals involved. Organizational leaders who see their purpose as educational, motivational, and relational may possess several of these characteristics and utilize a combination of these power types. The most effective leaders will adapt their approach to different situations and individuals to achieve desired outcomes. Understanding that one's merit is not localized in a job description is liberating.

Is leadership the same thing as power?

Dr. Martin Luther King wrote in his autobiography,

> Power, properly understood, is the ability to achieve purpose. It is the strength required to bring about social, political, or economic changes. In this sense power is not only desirable but necessary in order to implement the demands of love and justice. One of the greatest problems of history is that the concepts of love and power are usually contrasted as polar opposites. Love is identified with a resignation of power and power with a denial of love. What is needed is a realization that power without love is reckless and abusive and that love without power is sentimental and anemic. Power at its best is love implementing the demands of justice. Justice at its best is love correcting everything that stands against love.
>
> —*The Autobiography of Martin Luther King, Jr.*

APPLYING POWER TYPES TO DEAI PRACTICE

A good leader is one who internalizes Dr. King's words about love being necessary for justice. Leading with love and all that love means—empathy, compassion, forgiveness, kindness, time, commitment, and vulnerability—requires a diversity of leadership styles, kinds of power, and cultural awareness.

Everyone across the institution should be deputized to leadership in a DEAI context. It is the entire staff's responsibility to reduce or eradicate bias; remove prejudice from conversations; channel workflow to include, represent, and fully accept new and diverse voices, opinions, content, and work styles; and be intentionally anti-oppressive in the museum. When everyone is accountable, the organization can accomplish more, making use of everyone's powers and abilities. When this does not happen, unhappy museum constituents point to the people with the legitimate power (specifically the executive director and the director of diversity, equity, accessibility, and inclusion) and blame them for the state of affairs. Similarly, simply replacing a white leader with a person of color to diversity a leadership role does not amount to much if the DEAI strategy doesn't consider these kinds of power and how they can effect change.

AN EIGHTH INTERSECTIONAL POWER: PRIVILEGE

Privilege is defined as a special advantage or opportunity given to only certain people. In the late 1980s, Dr. Peggy McIntosh of Simmons College coined the term *white privilege* to illustrate what she was feeling when contemplating the differences between how Black people were regarded and treated compared with her own lived experiences as a white person. The privileges Dr. McIntosh references in her essay "Unpacking the Invisible Knapsack" are different from luxuries, such as flying first class or enjoying full-time maid services for life. The so-called privileges that white people generally have and BIPOC lack are the ability to be seen, heard, trusted, believed, safe, and respected. In an impressive but heartbreaking list of twenty-five to thirty scenarios, Dr. McIntosh talks about a white person's being fully represented, no matter the stature in life, versus a Black person's being subject to constant scrutiny and the pressure to prove meritorious, over and over ad nauseum, ad infinitum.

Whiteness is considered a privilege in this and other countries, particularly those shaped by historical and ongoing systems of white supremacy. People who are perceived as white experience certain advantages or benefits solely based on their perceived racial identity. This privilege is not inherent to being white as an individual but, rather, stems from the social construct of race and the power dynamics associated with it.

Here are some ways in which whiteness can confer privilege:

- People who identify as white or can pass as white often have greater representation and visibility in media, politics, education, and other influential spheres. This visibility can lead to increased social acceptance, relevance, validation, and influence. Historically, Black, Brown, and Native American people were prevented from participating or ascending in these spaces. Children were prevented from attending the same schools; the arts and media (and museums) were slow to add them to their performance schedules or rosters.
- White people have had and may still have greater access to quality education, health care, housing, employment opportunities, and financial resources due to laws, cultural mores, systemic biases, and discriminatory practices that disproportionately favor white individuals. General wealth and access to premium educational institutions have kept these institutions white, and these systems perpetuate themselves, allowing very little demographic change over time.
- Studies reveal that white people tend to have lower rates of arrest and conviction within the criminal justice system. They receive less harsh sentencing compared to individuals from marginalized racial or ethnic groups. The school-to-prison pipeline, a devastatingly named phenomenon describing the trajectory of boys in middle and high school who are disproportionately and unfairly punished in school and who too often land in correctional facilities over time, is a tragic reality for Black males.
- White people are less likely to experience racial profiling, harassment, or violence based solely on their racial identity. They feel safer and more secure in public spaces than people of other races, and they don't share the same fear of being targeted due to their race.
- Those who identify as white may face fewer challenges in navigating and assimilating into dominant cultural norms and institutions. Their cultural

practices and traditions are often seen as the default or norm, while those of marginalized communities may be marginalized or stigmatized.

- The emotional, physical, and psychological safety of these and others who have been marginalized can be supported and affirmed in museums, where, ideally, they might see, enjoy, and experience symbols and examples of their culture throughout.

White privilege does not mean that individual white people have not faced or don't currently face personal hardships. It merely acknowledges that systemic advantages exist for individuals who are perceived as white within systems shaped by white supremacy. Nothing changes if nothing changes. If a system, organization, group, or individual does nothing to change the oppressions that affirm white supremacy, the systems will not change.

Studying, acknowledging, understanding, and discussing white privilege is crucial in dismantling systemic racism and working toward a more just society. It involves actively challenging and disrupting systems of oppression, amplifying marginalized voices, and creating policies and practices that promote racial justice. Those with privilege and the powers most able to move others to action have the responsibility to help others in the ways Dr. King describes.

Calling attention to white privilege is not about blaming an individual today for what was done by ancestors centuries ago. It's about recognizing that harm and pain to Indigenous, Black, Brown, Asian, and other communities will continue if the people who still benefit from inequitable systems don't redress them using the power they still hold.

In an organization that is diversifying and planning every day to become increasingly more inclusive, this eighth context-heavy power must be addressed. Certainly, the calculus will be different for each museum, but depending on the leadership and staff demographics, their cultural competency, and their awareness of power, each instance of dominant culture versus category of marginalization will necessitate collaboration among people with different strengths and from different places on the organizational chart in thoughtful and courageous conversation.

GROUP EXERCISE: CHECKING OUR POWER AND PRIVILEGE

During a staff meeting or all-staff workshop, gather in small groups with this worksheet. Alternatively, you can answer the questions in your own journals and share at a later staff meeting.

1. Define each of the seven types of power in your own words as a group.

   a. Coercive power
   b. Reward power
   c. Legitimate power

    d. Referent power

    e. Expert power

    f. Informational power

    g. Connection power

2. As individuals, give examples of your using each of the seven kinds of power. If you do not have or use one or more of these, write n/a for not applicable.

    a. In your everyday life away from the museum

    b. At the museum in your job capacity as far as possible

3. Privilege as a power

    a. Consider whether you have been or are negatively impacted by white privilege. Give up to three examples.

    b. What can you do to give shelter, protect, amplify, or illuminate someone who does not have privilege?

    c. Write down as many other kinds of privilege you encounter in the museum setting, such as straight privilege, gender privilege (male), and others.

    d. Revisit questions (a) and (b) and give appropriate answers for each of the other privileges you are exploring.

4. Have a discussion with those in your small group about using the seven kinds of power and recognizing privilege.

    a. What can you do if your museum director and leadership team have certain kinds of power and not others, especially if you want to move critical components of your DEAI work forward? Brainstorm and explore possibilities together.

    b. What can you do to practice or strengthen your leadership skills and power types?

    c. How can you use your unique combinations of cultural strengths, power types, understanding of privilege, and empathy to become a more compassionate colleague who is a keen advocate for the DEAI initiative?

12

Collective Reckoning about Past and Present Oppression and Inequity in Museums

WHY STUDY THE HISTORY OF SLAVERY IN THE AMERICAS TOGETHER AS A MUSEUM?

In my years working directly with exhibitions and education in museums, I have been involved in planning for, writing about, presenting, and interpreting exhibitions having to do with the transatlantic slave trade; slavery in America; aspects of the Black American experience, and programs and exhibitions about various African and pan-African countries. It's interesting that in contrast, when preparing exhibitions about the United States or US culture in general, it's tacitly understood that the project is supposed to be of, about, and for white people only.

Exhibitions about Black people, Blackness, and people of color are thought to be negative, hostile, and divisive or profoundly less professional no matter the subject matter. Just calling up the idea of creating Black-themed design, art, or people-centered activities is seen as risky in museum spaces.

Bridget R. Cooks, professor of Art History and African American Studies at the University of California, Irvine, chronicles the struggle for representation and respect faced by Black American artists and curators over the decades since the first major museum of African American Art at the Chicago Art in 1927 in her book *Exhibiting Blackness: African Americans and the American Art Museum*. The tales of bias and exclusion are certainly troubling, but they align with the treatment of Black Americans in various systems and professions across the same periods of time.

It was slavery that enabled the foundation of systemic oppression based on race that still persists in America today. Scholars theorize that race was created because of slavery of those of black African extraction and descent: It was a way to mark who had the ostensible right to own another human and who was owned.

This reprehensible system was created to subjugate and enslave for life the seemingly inexhaustible supply of men, women, and children who were captured, sold, and distributed across the lands of the Americas, which included what is now the United States of America, the Caribbean, and Central and South America. It was not a bartering system among equals; it was people respecting each other as humans to fulfill a work contract, unequal though the indentured labor system might have been. The enslavement of Africans and anyone born to them was singularly inhumane—they were treated as property and denied human rights. They were not considered people at all by law or by society, and they were sold from household to household, whipped into compliance, and punished within an inch of their lives to be lessons to others. Children born on the plantations were taken from their own parents and sold to other properties and owner families because not even children belonged to their families of origin according to this pernicious system. When the enslaved women were raped, which was often, any resulting offspring were by law born into involuntary servitude. Defiant enslaved Africans and African Americans were sometimes shipped in the foulest of transports to one of the smaller Caribbean islands for extreme punishment before being returned to America after a peccadillo like trying to run away from ill-treatment or learning how to write English. They had no autonomy, no legal protections. They were forbidden from speaking their own languages.

African enslavement in America was a particularly entrenched system of oppression that lasted for centuries and served to divide, delineate, and dehumanize others based on skin color and other phenotypical characteristics. Race does not exist. It is a man-made construction and now is a social construct that we must disentangle to exist harmoniously and justly together.

BACK WHEN WE WERE DISHWASHERS

Back when we were dishwashers and lawnmowers,
Washing machines
Threshers and breast pumps
Back when we were branded with every household's name
A sizzling sear on a blistering black arm

Back when we were heavy machinery and household implements
We were expected to be seen, and not heard.
I could understand the frustration

When one of us didn't work right, or
Look good—
When some of us
Turned wrong,
Grew dull and bent

After all,
We were bought and paid for;
Could not be returned.

Our owners tried to fix us.
We came with no manuals.
(They'd looted us, after all)

So they tried to fix us
By boxing
our ears
Whipping us
into shape
Screwing half of us
Raw.
Cuffing us
Cauterizing us.

Still we worked as well as we could, considering.
Back then there was
No Customer Service window
No thirty-day window
No window in the quarters where we rested after daily use
No light
No air

Back when we were dishwashers
Our owners couldn't imagine us dreaming or scheming. Better they should
think we were just
Gins sitting around in the hot sun picking cotton
Or combines gossiping while harvesting tobacco
And sweet sugar cane.
Now that we've transformed
From machines
To full-fledged people
(Now that they've finally agreed we are)
Know this:

We didn't work for them; we worked for our lives
Now we don't have to answer to anyone else, or make others more comfortable by staying in place, tethered to a wall

Not speaking, just being serviceable and entertaining
Quietly in the background while you build a life.

We had hearts back then too—
Hearts and soft skin to touch
Arms to extend in a salute or embrace
Eyes that sparkled in fun and moistened when sad
A mouth to speak
And not just on cue,
Not just when spoken to.

Just
Like
Yours

You just didn't choose to believe it
You were so happy with your gleaming new machines

Back when we were dishwashers
© Cecile Shellman, 2020

Trevor Noah, inimitable South African comedian, writer, producer, and sage, has said: "In America, the history of racism is taught like this: 'There was slavery and then there was Jim Crow and then there was Martin Luther King Jr. and now it's done.'"

BORN A CRIME: STORIES FROM A SOUTH AFRICAN CHILDHOOD

It's sad but true that grown-ups in 21st-century United States of America know so little about our history. We know very little about the connectedness of our African-descended populations and those of our African-descended American cousins. We know so little about the atrocities of the system of chattel slavery because we would rather not hear anything unpleasant and are often too self-centered to comprehend how it affects us all.

The history of enslaved Black people in America and their progeny is an indubitably fascinating, frightening, and frustrating one. This history is American history, yet the very people who thrust the Americanness upon Black people are the ones who would deny their having done it and deny them their humanness as well. Not only would they deny their humanity; they would exploit it, benefit from it, and continue to deny it for generations.

Claude McKay's "I, too, sing America" was penned to express that the lonely, eloquent song of an unclaimed Black son remains unheard on the basis of color alone. The throat on which Derek Chauvin knelt defiantly was a Black throat, as were the bodies of so many Black people throughout the last several hundred years yearning to prove they are wanted in the only home they have been forced to know. It's a shameful history that seems too bitter and fantastical to countenance, so many turn away and hope it will disappear if ignored.

Author Resmaa Menaken posits that generational trauma about racism lies deep in the body and that Americans—no matter the racial or ethnic imprint—carry this burden throughout life. After all, he says in a brilliant Medium essay, "How Racism Began as White-on-White Violence, May 2, 2018": "When the Europeans came to America after enduring 1,000 years of plague, famine, inquisitions and crusades they brought much of their resilience, much of their brutality, and I believe, a great deal of their trauma with them."

Menaken refers to the brutality of punishments exacted in medieval Europe, where violent crusades, inquisitions, kidnappings, and ruthless torture were de rigueur. So, too, in the so-called New World were the whippings, poker-scorching branding of human skin, and cutting off ears. He speaks of bones being crushed as punishment, recounting the tale of an eighty-year-old white man being dragged and crushed by rocks. Until the late 1600s, punishments such as these were meted out to any bodies, Black, white, Native, that crossed and disobeyed wealthy white landowners. Enslaved Africans lived and worked alongside indentured workers who were non-landholding white people as well as workers from various Native American tribes. Occasionally, the workers would revolt due to abysmal conditions and treatment.

Eventually, white plantation workers of modest or dire need were given stolen parcels of Native land to farm in exchange for their loyalty to the plantation owners and became the newer peasant class that had privilege, earned money, owned property, and were white no matter their geographic origins or language. Eventually, it became exceedingly clear who the white people were—who had privilege whether or not they owned land—and who were Black, loathsome, filthy. Carl Linnaeus's taxonomy and various religious texts contributed to the shaming and dehumanizing of Black people from the African continent who were routinely stolen by the British, Portuguese, Spanish, Dutch, and French and transported to America. More than ten million African people were eventually forcibly transported across the Atlantic over the course of three hundred years from various regions of Africa, kidnapped in the dead of night or sold by their own people. If their passage was completed, after months of sloshing around a small filthy prison cell of a hull for months, branded, barely fed, stripped, whipped, and broken.

Most of them were sent to the so-called West Indies, or the Caribbean—Jamaica, Haiti, and Cuba in particular—and to Brazil, which received the largest number of enslaved Africans, approximately five million, and is still the country with the world's largest African-descended population outside of the African continent to this day. The enslaved persons in the Caribbean turned sugarcane into granulated sugar, molasses, and rum, which was sold and even pirated worldwide at high cost. Other Central and South American countries purchased enslaved Africans to cultivate sugar, coffee, and cacao; extract diamonds; mine emeralds and gold; perform domestic labor; construct roads and bridges; and even provide military service. North America (the areas that became the United States) received only 400,000 people from Africa, and they were primarily scattered across the Southern states to pick cotton and farm tobacco and other crops.

With their different skin colors, hair texture, language, and shared customs, the Africans were easy scapegoats for the Europeans in America to treat them with contempt, savagery, and disfavor. Sadly, this treatment was enabled, aided, and justified by slave holders' interpretation of the church's rhetoric. They'd done this before: the Carib Indians and aboriginal peoples of Central and South America were brutalized in the name of God during the Crusades.

The black skin of the new African laborers became just another divider demonstrating the tropes of holy writ.

This brutality was transferred onto a newer peasant class, and eventually, as chattel slavery spread across the Americas due to the transatlantic slave trade with the colonies of Spain, France, Portugal, the Dutch Empires, and England, the Black body primarily was mistreated in horrific fashion as race was born.

It is a history that is perpetuated into the present and future the more some try to erase it. It is far more, and far more profound, than a few units in middle school could ever teach. Many individuals and groups have visited severe harm on others they define as different across the centuries and miles. The major difference is with the enslavement of Black people and the massive wealth created off the labor of their bodies and spilling of their blood, a bleak dehumanization was codified into law and culture, persisting into the present day.

There are politicians, parents, and principals nationwide who want to destroy curricula that teach Black history in a thorough and incisive way. Instead, they try to reduce the deprivation and ignominy of slavery to a phrase or two hidden in a textbook about happy indentured workers surviving despite mildly unpleasant circumstances. Some jurisdictions and districts in our country have disallowed teaching full and true stories about that and other systems that favor and protect the wealthy and white while marginalizing and further impoverishing people of color and people of fewer financial means. A 2018 study from the Southern Poverty Law Center, "Teaching Hard History: American Slavery," found that 56 percent of teachers polled weren't happy with their textbooks and almost 40 percent said their state offered little or no support for teaching about slavery.

Critically examining racism is not about wondering whether individual white and BIPOC people are currently interacting, being pleasant or kind to each other, or working side by side; whether or not that is so, the effect of systemic oppression as seen from the historic roots and eventual branches is blatant. Were there individual people of color who succeeded in various ways despite cultural opprobrium, social mores, and laws that extended well into the 20th century and beyond? Absolutely. The larger system, however, as established in the 1700s, was created to enrich and support the separation of races and the political, social, and economic successes of one over the other.

Many other kinds of oppression in the United States follow the same alarming ancestry, with roots in a majority group with privilege knowingly or through tradition excluding, ignoring, or harming those who are not. Whether it's people who are nondisabled refusing to make space for those who have disabilities or cis heterosexual males benefiting from superior status accorded by traits outside of their control—we can all find lessons in history that point to the origins of such beginnings. Knowing the origins can help some people recognize when there is no there there—that things don't have to be the way they are and that people of color, sexual minorities, gender minorities, people with disabilities, and others whose differences make a difference as marginalized people can find comfort, redress, and justice in an imperfect world.

This is true also for a museum. Analyzing a museum's history and seeing where it originated to enthrall the privileged at the expense of the marginalized is a good exercise in understanding patterns, practices, power, and traditions in today's museums that perpetuate that behavior. In the same way that researching the transatlantic slave trade and the enslavement of African-descended people in America elucidates the irony and tragedy of gentrification, so, too, can awareness of other colonizer and supremacy behavior alert us to patterns to avoid or ameliorate today.

Museums can bring alive the unpalatable palette of shades, colors, tints, and hues modeled just so to fashion built environments that recreate scenes from a plantation great house or print large facsimiles of slave auction broadsheets for visitors to handle and see for themselves. Museums can preserve and present shackles and chains that once encircled the feet of captured children. They can carefully and reverently place these sacred objects on pillowed mounts, under glass vitrines and with contextualized labels written thoughtfully yet factually for a full understanding of the objects' import. They can educate in age-appropriate ways. Elucidation, not erasure, is the key to informed consensual learning.

When institutions insist to communities of color and others they have marginalized throughout hundreds of years of history: "We don't see (color); you're exactly like us," they are saying, "We don't see the circumstances under which we are here together today, and we don't accept the fraught histories that combined to create somewhat unseen inequities that we still are required to fix." We cannot fix what we cannot face. Unless museums become humble, vulnerable, collaborative, and justice minded, they will not be in the business of repairing the past. They will only continue to reframe it in more tolerable, more palatable ways. They will checklist themselves into safe spaces meant for others who truly need protection from harm.

There are lessons to learn from other heritages, other branches of the Strange Fruit enslavement tree: the United States was not the last to abolish slavery, yet it was among the last to relinquish its political and legal hold on formalized prejudice and segregation. Other countries with slavery in their past acknowledge people of color and their contribution proudly in everyday life and heritage: The samba, feijoada, and capoeira of Brazil are considered fully Brazilian and not just oddities consumed by the descendants of the formerly enslaved Africans. By contrast, Black and other minoritized people of the United States of America still struggle to be accepted as Americans and have their cultural contributions be thought of as Brazilian as pão de queijo. While things are improving—at the time of this writing hip-hop is being celebrated for its fifty years as an American music genre—we still have far to go.

In the United States, there were de facto and de jure attempts to reinstitute slavery despite having abolished it or at every point, terrorize Black people so that they felt small, unsafe, undeserving, and ineffectual at best, hunted and despised at worst. Miscegenation between Black and white people in particular was a present and pernicious fear among white people in America such that rules and laws were created to prevent Black people from even looking into the eyes of or smiling at a white man, woman, or child. Even polite society and their churches countenanced this particular kind of segregation, claiming to want to protect unborn children.

Jim Crow laws of the South soon became cultural practices that everyone followed to ensure the separate but equal model that would persist for decades. In 1955 when young Emmett Till's Black battered body was pictured above the fold of the *Chicago Tribune*, some people began to see the danger of that model. What was done in the shadows was now, through the media, up close and personal for thousands of people to view, here and abroad.

Museums must do more than research and acknowledge. Many museums present the stories of enslavement very well, including the National Museum of African American History and Culture in Washington, DC, to the Whitney Plantation in Los Angeles, the Old Slave Mart Museum in South Carolina, and the Museum of the African Diaspora in San Francisco. Scores of other museums present exhibitions and programs about African enslavement periodically throughout their annual slate of exhibitions and activities. They tell the stories of tribulations but also of revolt, revolution, escape, hope, and emancipation.

Even more importantly, however, museums must overturn and rebuild their fraught history into an open and accepting future, one that not only accepts everyone in a benign way but demonstrates that some of its own practices are rooted in contemptible histories and revolutionize all of these. The queries now for a museum in the 21st century become How to repatriate? How to resolve this? How to perform this reconciliation with intention, vulnerability, and intent?

Museums interpret history and support the telling of it through objects and primary source documents. They can and should be the primary truth tellers of these unsavory stories. It's incumbent on all museums—not just the history ones that by charter interpret 17th- to 20th-century stories—to investigate and allow untold stories to reappear in our lexicons and in our museum halls. Small efforts to do so, such as hiring living interpreters who reintroduce the lived experience of people of color in colonial life and beyond, help to avoid erasure of Black, Indigenous, and People of Color and invite further questions about how Black and white people lived together despite law and custom.

People trust museums to tell the truth. Museums have a stated duty to preserve, study, and display valuable historical and artistic objects related to our heritage. We rely on museums to interpret and contextualize stories of our past and present; we hope that museums can facilitate lifelong learning for individuals of all ages and interests. Visitors trust that their museums—especially those with nonprofit status—are entirely trustworthy and are employing the best of their research and knowledge to serve with modest intent rather than to sensationalize the sacred for public gain.

Museums can fill in the gaps for K–12 schools, universities, and other organizations that should but don't face American history. African American history is American history.

When museums investigate their own stories, they may find that they, too, are unwittingly upholding the same disagreeable practices that allowed wealthy white people to flourish and People of Color, those with few means, and others to be relegated to the margins. They may find that supposedly benign practices, such as favoring the founder's descendants or friends of descendants to be a specialized group at the museum over time, receiving unearned and highly prestigious status, is a practice that is highly exclusionary and supports segregation. Were any of your museum founders People of Color after 1962? If not, it's highly unlikely that they intended their legacy committees to be peopled by those of color. Keeping those kinds of exclusionary practices and holding them in high regard might indicate that the museum is unserious about justice reforms. It would be the same as keeping a white-only golf course long after such constructs were socially disallowed and impugned.

What can museums learn about white supremacy culture—the culture that allowed for the creation of race and the dehumanizing of nonwhite people? How can you—as museum teams, exhibition creators, community conveners, and individuals dedicated to justice—demonstrate that your DEAI practice is subdermal and that it is a life-changing, life-giving endeavor?

The work of Dr. Tema Okun, sometimes maligned for its naming white supremacy culture as a universal ongoing reality, is nevertheless brilliant in its description of certain behaviors and habits that lead to maintaining a majority status quo. In White Supremacy Culture, the reader is asked to consider whether oppressive behaviors are motivating or limiting, why these behaviors exist at all, and who benefits and who is harmed by the behaviors.

White Supremacy Culture is about valuing white people and their safety, comfort, and ascendency above all else. The words *white supremacy* invoke fear and bring to mind instances of extreme physical violence by racists who despise and seek to eradicate nonwhite humans. Okun's writings have taught that the violence of erasure and the insidiousness of excluding, ignoring, and repressing nonwhite voices and desires are also patently evil. It's not just a bad business practice; it's perpetuating the idea that some of us do not belong in spaces that should be inhabited and enjoyed by all. We are humans too. We love our families. We work hard. We pay our taxes. As Sojourner Truth asked, "Ain't I a woman?

SYSTEMS

We learn to accept behavior because those around us see no harm in living unlivable customs. They see no harm or believe that the harm is less important than their survival within the system. We learn that certain systems and systemic behavior are OK because the behavior is not challenged, or we want to protect the system because it's related to someone or something that is beloved to us, or we still value and contribute to it. Many of us—perhaps all of us—are guilty of this in some way. Every system is designed to obtain the results it gets.

IT'S NOT JUST SYSTEMS—IT'S PEOPLE

We should not be so quick as to excuse people for following the system owing to human weakness. Those who throw their hands in the air and claim that this is our culture, after all, and nothing can be done. It is our responsibility to do the right thing. There are also people within oppressive systems who claim that because the oppression isn't happening to them, it is not happening or not important. Even people whose own ancestors have faced these oppressions can be dismissive of the idea of redress because they haven't seen it work in the real world. The blood of native peoples of the Americas, enslaved Africans in revolt, women burned at the stake for living as women among ignorant people, men who love men forbidden from thriving as their true selves—calls out for justice and demands an answer. All of the injustices and more are maintained the longer it takes for people in power to do nothing.

We must think about power differently if we are to make any lasting changes in any systemic anti-oppression endeavor. All of us have some power, and those with the most power need to work contrary to their inkling to isolate and delegate. Working together in ways that strengthen communication, elucidate problems, highlight solutions, and improve relationships is a good start to breaking down hierarchical barriers and establishing trust.

It can begin as simply as listening and learning from people who are different from you or people whose viewpoints you have never heard or considered. Reconsider what it means to be an expert and allow community and staff members to be meaningful contributors to the efforts of researching, reconstructing, and reworking together.

We need to be brave. We need to be courageous about relating difficult stories even if those stories and their telling incriminate us of our unwillingness to engage. We need to be courageous enough to face other examples of suffering and injustice all over the world and to resolve ourselves to combat it wherever it occurs. We need to be brave enough to make restitution, to show true remorse, and to reflect on our repentance for things that can never fully be forgiven. We might not have been the direct instigators, but the more we ignore the effects of slavery and racism and the less we deal with society's burden because of it, the more we are culpable. Learning about slavery in the ways a museum can teach it helps us to honor the enslaved. Learning this history can profoundly inform current debates about pressing social ills that we can eventually redress through the justice system.

DECOLONIZING THE MUSEUM

Colonization in a museum system sense is related to racism and white supremacy, but it is specifically focused on repatriating the material elements of culture that were stolen by the majority culture in America and in museums. Decolonization entails restoring the sovereignty, dignity, and rightful place of the indigenous or other oppressed people within the system and on returning religious and traditional lands, artifacts, language, symbols, and resources. While it also looks at origin stories and locates intrinsic racist practices, decolonizing demands the truth telling about the stolen people and things and restoring human, intellectual, and financial resources in museums and calling out their malign past. Decolonization and repatriation go hand in hand.

Colonialism and white supremacy intersect in challenging systems of power and confronting both past and present harm. Both serve the purpose of acknowledging harm and restoring dignity to previously marginalized peoples. If anti-racism is the repentance for wrongdoing, decolonization is the restoration for what was stolen even though, of course, in real terms, such as restoration, can never happen.

Where anti-racism can start with looking at personal connections, examining bias, and reckoning with personal and systemic acts of exclusion based on race and ethnicity, decolonization can be the material manifestation of those anti-racist intentions.

EXERCISE: EXPLORING DECOLONIZATION PRACTICES IN MUSEUMS

This worksheet is designed to encourage museum employees to reflect on and explore decolonization practices within your organization. Please take the time to answer the following questions and engage in critical self-reflection.

1. Defining Decolonization for Your Museum:

   a. Define decolonization in the context of museums. Remember that for different kinds of museums, there are different kinds of actions that should be considered or imagined.
   b. Why is decolonization important for museums? What are the potential benefits?

2. Assessing Current Best and Worst Practices:

   a. Reflect on your museum's current practices and narratives. Are they inclusive and representative of diverse perspectives and communities? Why or why not?
   b. Identify any potential biases or gaps in your museum's collections, exhibitions, or programming. How do these biases or gaps perpetuate colonial narratives or power imbalances?

3. Engaging with Communities:

   a. Describe any existing initiatives or efforts your museum has undertaken to engage with communities and include diverse voices. How effective have these initiatives been? Can you understand why? Are there cultural barriers that need to be overcome?
   b. How can your museum further collaborate with communities to ensure their active participation and representation in exhibitions and programming?

4. Repatriation and Restitution:

   a. Research and discuss any instances where your museum holds cultural artifacts or human remains that may be subject to repatriation or restitution. How does your museum approach these issues?
   b. What steps can your museum take to address historical injustices and work toward repatriation or restitution?

5. Staff Diversity and Inclusion:

   a. Evaluate the diversity within your museum's staff and leadership positions. Are there any barriers or challenges to achieving a more diverse workforce? Is your internal museum culture such that the staff members describe themselves as being colonized, brutalized, or ill-treated?

b. What strategies can your museum implement to recruit, retain, and support a more diverse staff?

6. Action Plan:

a. Based on your reflections and responses to the previous questions, outline three actionable steps your museum can take to further decolonize its practices and promote inclusivity.

b. How can you personally contribute to these efforts? What role can you play in promoting decolonization within your museum?

IMPORTANT CONSIDERATIONS TO MAKE WHEN INITIATING YOUR DEAI PLANS: COMPENSATION CONSIDERATIONS

Never forget that the forced labor of millions of people of African people, without pay, had lasting effects on these enslaved individuals and their descendants. In addition to generational poverty, consequences include generational trauma, social stigma, bias against people of color, pay inequity, and mental health concerns.

Museums are not known for highly compensating their employees, which is problematic when discussions about DEAI occur. If your museum is serious about its DEAI work, you may want to think about the implications of championing inclusion and equity while maintaining practices that solidify unfair pay structures, including the extraordinary gap between the executive's salary and that of the lowest paid worker. More transparency needs to happen, and habits that discourage wage increases must cease. In some museums, a curatorial assistant can begin earning $20,000 per annum while an executive director can earn close to $1M in 2023.

When museums consider funding a DEAI leadership position, they should begin with the notion that these positions must be compensated equitably. Paying DEAI leaders and professionals less than other roles with similar levels of responsibility will undermine the effect of your DEAI initiative considerably.

PRIORITIZING THE WORK

Recognizing the value and importance of diversity and inclusion efforts is crucial. Investing in these initiatives, including compensating the team responsible for driving them, budgeting appropriately for an office responsible for its administration, monitoring your accessibility and disability-justice efforts and updating as needed, can demonstrate the organization's commitment to creating an inclusive workplace.

EXPERTISE AND SPECIALIZED SKILLS

Realize that diversity and inclusion work requires specific knowledge, skills, and expertise. A staff member's identity or cultural upbringing alone will not qualify someone for an advisory or supervisory position on a DEAI team. Leadership, conflict management, cultural awareness, crisis management skills and deep knowledge about intercultural competence, social science, civics, public policy, communications, and government regulations (such as with the Americans with Disabilities Act and other disability-justice regulations at the federal and municipal levels) are excellent competencies to consider. A director of diversity and inclusion position is no small appointment, and the position should be paid well. Compensation can be a way to attract and retain talented professionals who can effectively lead and implement key diversity and inclusion strategies.

TASK FORCES AND COMMITTEES ALSO REQUIRE EXTENSIVE TIME AND EFFORT

Diversity and inclusion work often involves significant time and effort, including research, training, policy development, and ongoing initiatives. Providing additional compensation to those who serve on diversity committees and other standing committees related to your approach can acknowledge and compensate for the extra workload and dedication required. Offering additional compensation can serve as an incentive and motivation for team members to go above and beyond their regular responsibilities. It can also help attract individuals who are passionate about diversity and inclusion and willing to invest their time and energy into these efforts as the years pass and new members are brought onto the teams.

Ensuring equity and fairness in compensation is essential. If other teams or roles with similar levels of responsibility and impact receive additional compensation, it may be appropriate to extend the same consideration to the diversity and inclusion team.

Compensation can reflect the organization's values and priorities. If diversity and inclusion are core values, compensating the team responsible for driving these initiatives can align with the organization's commitment to creating an inclusive workplace culture.

13

Accessibility in Museums

AN APPEAL FOR JUSTICE, A CASE FOR COMPASSION

A remarkable event occurred on March 13, 1990. It was a lovely spring day in Washington, DC. More than 1,000 marchers made their way from the White House to the US Capitol Building to continue a demonstration demanding that Congress pass the Americans with Disabilities Act.

That day, a memorable embodiment of the struggle for civil rights was beautifully and spontaneously enacted on the steps of the Capitol Building. Now known as the Capitol Crawl, this action refers to the coordinated effort in which about seventy-five people with disabilities affecting their mobility abandoned their mobility aids, hurling themselves onto the eighty stone steps leading up to the Capitol Building and proceeded to climb—face down, back to the building, arms grabbing and fingers cradling the rolled edges of the cement stair steps, whatever it took until inch by inch, step after excruciatingly painful step, they reached the landing. They were cheered on by hundreds of other activists chanting fervent refrains about their hope that an Americans with Disabilities Act would finally be passed. The bill had stalled for months in Congress. An ADA ruling would mean that civil rights for people with disabilities would be enshrined in law. Discrimination on the basis of disability would be illegal in employment, state and local government, public accommodations, commercial facilities, transportation, and telecommunications.

As the dozens of protesters crawled slowly up the steps—each one with a unique and painful story of disability to tell, even the youngest crawler at age eight—photographs and video were taken to memorialize the powerful, sacred images. This was not just theater. There was no other way for these people to ascend the gradient of the Capitol Building—or any other government building.

Ramps were not commonplace on any buildings in as late as 1990, yet if ever a person who used a wheelchair were summoned for jury duty or to pay a fine in person, they were still required to do so even if it meant being carried or dragged by others. There were no personal computers in widespread use and no smartphones available through which a form could be filled out or renewal could be processed. Most municipal tasks required individuals to appear in person with proof of identification, some of which was hard for people with mobility disabilities to attain.

When the crawlers reached the top, the testimonials commenced. The first Deaf president of Gallaudet University, the nation's first university for Deaf and hard-of-hearing students in Washington, DC, was a passionate and persuasive presenter. Others talked of trials recent and pressing, of long-term discrimination and barriers to access.

Four months later, in July 1990, the Americans with Disabilities Act was signed into law by President George H. W. Bush.

As we know from other examples of civil rights struggles and legislation, the story does not end there and not with a guaranteed happily ever after.

According to the Centers for Disease Control and Prevention (CDC), people with disabilities represent the largest minority group in the United States. About 26 percent of adults in the United States have some form of disability, including disabilities related to mobility, cognition, hearing, vision, and independent living. When museums think of welcoming visitors, are they including people who have disabilities?

> Historically, society has tended to isolate and segregate individuals with disabilities, and, despite some improvements, such forms of discrimination against individuals with disabilities continue to be a serious and pervasive social problem.
> Discrimination against individuals with disabilities persists in such critical areas as employment, housing, public accommodations, education, transportation, communication, recreation, institutionalization, health services, voting, and access to public services.
> —US Equal Employer Opportunity Commission

A museum is considered a Title III entity according to the Americans with Disabilities Act, which is one of several regulations upholding the civil and human rights of people with disabilities in the United States. Title III does the following:

> Prohibit(s) discrimination on the basis of disability in the activities of places of public accommodations (businesses that are generally open to the public and that fall into one of 12 categories listed in the ADA, such as restaurants, movie theaters, schools, day care facilities, recreation facilities, and doctors' offices) and requires newly constructed or altered places of public

accommodation—as well as commercial facilities (privately owned, nonresidential facilities such as factories, warehouses, or office buildings)—to comply with the ADA Standards. (https://www.ada.gov/ada_title_III.htm)

Despite the clear instruction and legal mandate to cease discrimination and provide various forms of access, museums and other Title III organizations are sometimes negligent or unwilling to meet the basic thresholds of accommodation or procrastinate in repairing or building adequate structures to make their visitors comfortable and safe.

Museum staff report feeling overwhelmed, shy, confused, ignorant of the rules, or in some cases, put upon, when asked why accessibility is not of higher priority. While it does take time to evaluate and strategize a workable solution for your museum's accessibility needs, it's not just a courteous gesture or the right thing to do—it's the law! There is no debate of whether your museum should have an accessibility plan; it's how to implement it.

A primary consideration should be to keep the word *accessibility* in your initiative's acronym. Whether you use DEAI, IDEA, or something else, please don't exclude *accessibility*. We name what we dare to face, and if we drop *accessibility* from the established DEAI moniker, we unwittingly communicate that accessibility and disability justice are either of less importance or will happen naturally just by dint of doing all the other important things involved in diversity, equity, inclusion, and anti-oppression strategies.

With one in four adults in the United States identifying as people with disabilities, it's highly likely that most visitors to a museum and most staff will personally know people who need accommodations and assistance to navigate private and public spaces. Museums and other Title III entities are required to provide reasonable accommodations. Some museums err on the side of ease and thrift when deciding when and whether to do so. This is highly problematic, however. Museums should be gracious and generous in their provision of accommodations, realizing that the environment is further disabling someone who is not able to traverse it due to barriers or neglect; it's the museum's responsibility, not a rote courtesy, to supply that accommodation.

Some examples of reasonable accommodations for museums follow:

- Providing accessible museum tours through the use of visual descriptions, verbal descriptions, tactile objects, ASL interpretation, Deaf-blind interpretation, and technology. Note that the use of technology as a solution is not one-size-fits-all solution. There are times when technology can further alienate people who wish to be fully included.
- Providing sound amplification for lectures and tours. If you advertise the provision of sound amplification as an accessibility accommodation, make sure to have the equipment available at all times, in working condition, and cleaned after each use. Make sure that all staff who will be using and

caring for the equipment know how to use it. There are various devices and apparatuses that can aid those who require amplification, but no two situations are alike. Make sure to communicate with the potential user to understand what is needed.

- Using closed and open captions in video presentations, both those produced by the museum and those curated into exhibitions. Artists should be aware that the museum's standards require accessibility provisions and should bear that in mind when creating work for exhibitions.
- Providing wheelchairs for those with mobility disabilities. Many museums offer wheelchairs that are manually operated.
- Providing chairs to sit on during long tours, including portable stools and folding seats that are easy to operate.
- Using plain language for exhibit text, websites, and marketing materials. Remember that those with cognitive disabilities visit museums, too, and that language—even for those who speak and write in the majority language—can be a barrier to full inclusion as well as a disability concern.
- Using apps and websites to preview the exhibit spaces, museum halls, and pathways of access and egress.
- Providing sensory-friendly programming and sensory-friendly days.

Note that these opportunities should not be considered or marketed for revenue-generating purposes because these are accommodations. For any of the accommodations listed, as well as others you may contemplate, no charge should be associated therewith.

How informed are you about your museum spaces? Do you know what it takes to get to the front entrance of the building? Here's an exercise that you can do alone or with your museum colleagues.

SERVICE OUTLINE EXERCISE

As you look around your museum spaces or if you can close your eyes and visualize what your campus looks like:

1. Can you remember how an everyday visitor would enter the museum property, find the admission doors, and approach the museum? Can you describe it in four sentences?
2. Think of the same scenario in four different seasons at the museum even if you don't have vast differences in weather conditions every quarter.
3. What can you do to make each entrance of the museum more accessible to people who have mobility challenges? Instead of imagining that they are entering the museum, think of them as if they were on the Capitol Crawl, entering your building to make a speech about museums and their need for greater attention to accessibility and disability rights.

4. Remember that even one step up into a room or doorframe, one uneven side-walk panel, one overgrown or broken curb cut, or one displaced stone on a path can mean a big difference to who can and who can't enter the museum.
5. Now, do the same for every five hundred feet of the museum, imagining it in every direction as well as every room in the museum. This is not an accessibility audit. Rather, it is a service design outline. It's an outline from your point of view and your experience whether or not you are experiencing a disability. Check the drawing or narrative with your memory of it after you have recorded it.
6. Convene a small group of people with disabilities, comprising people with whom you already have some kind of relationship, and invite them to come to the museum for a focus group event, making sure to physically meet them at any of the problematic entrances. Have them participate in top museum activities and then enjoy a talk about what their experiences at the museum are. Tell them about the service outline exercise you con-ducted and inquire about their own experiences. Ask how the experience could be better, whether and when personal interactions or physical sup-ports would be more helpful for guiding them through the museum, and strive to understand their fears and eventually resolve their concerns about visiting museum spaces.

DESIGNING AND MAINTAINING ACCESSIBLE SPACES FOR MUSEUMS

It's often said that museums should design, build, and maintain physically accessible spaces for museums to ensure that everyone, regardless of bodily ability, can enjoy and learn from exhibits and displays. While that is certainly true, because some other people may find ramps and railings helpful, framing accessibility in terms of disability justice is a more appropriate way of under-standing the importance of building accessibility. It is far more than just a design choice. To someone with a disability, a streamlined contemporary build-ing with wide, open spaces; clean lines; and bright lights might yet be a veritable fortress. If the floors are slanted to the wrong degree or the open spaces have flooring that is too slippery, too rough, or covered in mats that are not perma-nently tacked down, the ground could be unstable and hazardous.

Remember, too, that abiding by federal standards such as the Americans with Disabilities Act is not the same as following the building code or expect-ing the builders, contractors, and inspectors of an edifice to accurately and regularly meet the standards that will assure compliance. If a doorway is not wide enough for a wheelchair to enter even by a fraction of an inch, wheelchair users will not be able to pass through. If a door pushes in rather than pulls out, that, too, can make a difference for someone with mobility disabilities and sight disabilities and those without limbs, hands, or digits.

Consult your region's Americans with Disabilities Act website for current newsletters, updated legal information, and standards.

14

Developing and Implementing Bespoke and Individualized DEAI Plans

As your museum teams become more trusting and conversant with each other about matters related to diversity, equity, accessibility, and inclusion, you will have a better idea about what your values and beliefs are, how realistic your DEAI goals might be, and whether you have the capacity to implement the objectives you choose to set. Carve out several minutes from each scheduled staff, team, or sub-team meeting to concentrate on writing the plan together, focusing on hearing what people are learning through their own reading, journaling exercises, observations, peer shares, and feedback from others outside the institution.

If your museum team members have continued to engage in self-reflection and note-taking, as well as conferring with team members about how to solve challenging issues pertaining to equity and inclusion, they are developing their critical thinking muscles in an environment of empathy and trust. To develop your own individualized DEAI and anti-oppression plan, team members must display the kind of vulnerability that encourages them to divulge their foibles, fears, and feelings. This is the only way for an organization to be honest with themselves and their constituents about their social stance and duty to the community.

A first step in devising your plan is creating an internal mission statement about DEAI. This is different from your public relations plan or statement, which is usually more aspirational, more rote, and less prescriptive in nature. The internal plan is a compilation of your collective emotions, thoughts, and beliefs about issues related to DEAI and anti-oppression; what you know you are capable of; whom you can count on as internal and external champions; what your immediate priorities are; and what your vision for the future entails. If that sounds like a lot—it is! It can also be accomplished in a few paragraphs, responding to typical newscaster questions: who, what, when, why, where, and how regarding DEAI.

For instance, from a number of rousing discussions about the strategic plan, an exhibit opening, or roles of staff members and leaders, the museum's purpose can be suggested: To be the best resource on 20th-century clothespins in the nation! To be the most aesthetically interesting museum of clothespin art. To convene the best scholars of clothespin usage and design. Relative to DEAI, another team member might point out that the museum does not now do a good job of telling stories of anything besides those who profit off the clothespin industry. Another person might mention that might be a good opportunity to begin to tell more diverse stories—diverse both in the context of more numerous and varied as well as regarding people whose differences are important for the museum to recognize and include. After this, comments about representation, compensation, privilege, and visibility might ensue, followed by opinions about how to solicit and actively enjoin community member input. Write all of these ideas, questions, conclusions, and more questions in your weeks-long search for meaning in your DEAI statement of purpose.

Following this conversation, an initial statement might be crafted that acknowledges the museum is in its early stages of understanding and provision of meaningful DEAI strategies, but based on its earnest desires to be for all people and to tell stories of those who had not had the chance previously to speak for themselves, this is now something you will be engaged in doing.

Together, you might decide that while there are numerous stories you could recount through exhibitions and programs, it might be more worthwhile to start building relationships and helping smaller, less-resourced museums with their DEAI goals in the process. You might find value in collaborating with other clothespin museums across the country instead of conserving your research and feeling proud about being the biggest and best clothespin museum around. You might also realize in the course of conversation that your customary stance is to use public relations to crow constantly about what you do well instead of taking time to listen to feedback and gain an understanding of what you do not do well at all. You may want to add this to your statement as a humble discovery as you are learning what it means to be fully inclusive and anti-oppressionist within a multicultural, transforming environment. This may also be a new way you engage with the public, deferentially stating outwardly that you do not know everything about clothespins and their meaning to others but that you are learning and welcome contributions as opportunities to build knowledge and enhance culture together.

After the purpose statement is written, staff, leaders, and volunteers from the same work groups should reconvene and work out the kinds of tasks and strategies relative to the main goals and what they need from each other to achieve their interdepartmental aims. For instance, as all the education staff regroup, they might realize they don't have the community connections they need to be successful in developing relevant programs or they need to collaborate more often and earlier with the exhibitions department if they are going to seamlessly include programs for people with disabilities.

Next, the group should reconvene as smaller groups as often as possible over time during the course of their work projects to decide what to include, what to add, and whether the promises made are too lofty, challenging but doable, or the bare minimum. Every goal should have action items assigned, and every action item should have personnel responsible.

The group should also hear feedback from people who are confused by or outright against a DEAI focus or reframing of the museum's practices. They should have the opportunity to air their beliefs, be heard, and learn with others. This conversation should be respectful but should not demean or denigrate those who are vulnerable and marginalized.

The museum leadership and DEAI working group can also assert that this is the policy of the museum—to have, to enact, to comply with, and to promote strategies that protect and reduce harm to people who have been marginalized. It's the duty of every staff member to seek greater understanding and be in accordance with the museum's mission because their efforts in DEAI activity throughout the year will be counted for or against them just as any other workplace behavior would. That said, resolving concerns is an inclusive and kind behavior, a good practice to include.

Note that this process will take weeks, months, even years. Developing and refining your museum's purpose with a DEAI/justice focus and consolidating on a single page will not be an easy task. It's impossible to tell how long it will take your museum to accomplish this—it depends on the museum's culture; your dedication to the work; your thoughtful leadership and exceptional employees; and your willingness to collaborate with everyone in the museum and give them voice, allowing them the power of representation.

If there is a pressing need to supply an outward-facing statement for your website, for press releases, or for other reasons, write a statement in your museum's typical format and voice that is based on your internal work. Don't copy, contrive, or co-opt other organizations' material.

As you create and refine your own internal statement, however, you should continue to do all the things that you know you ought to as an emerging DEAI-focused institution. These other tasks will fall in place along the timeline as you authentically, purposefully, and collaboratively engage with your colleagues and the outer community.

WHAT DOES A MUSEUM THAT VALUES DEAI AS A JUSTICE DRIVER DO? YOU LISTEN AND LEARN FROM EACH OTHER WITH GRACE AND CARE

Listen to each other's written statements and vocal conversations about hopes, successes, doubts, beliefs, and fears. Practice listening without judgment and allow your colleagues to speak, especially those who don't ordinarily have a chance to speak openly in the presence of fellow workmates.

Pay attention to how others respond and how much agreement or disagreement there might be in the group. Don't be afraid of disagreement or conflict. No two humans will have the same opinions, and it's a wonderful thing to be human, to have the chance to be human and live in this world as a confident, sentient being. Do others among your peers have similar beliefs—so similar that it's eerie? That could be a good thing in terms of shared values, but consider this: What might very close beliefs or widely differing ones mean to the museum? Could there be affinity bias happening in the hiring and management levels to value sameness and to manufacture an environment of calm to avoid conflict? What could wildly differing viewpoints and consensus-stopping disagreements mean?

Explore your museum's history together. If there's an employee who fancies themselves a casual museum historian, can you consider adding that person to your DEAI team to document and archive the cultural changes that are occurring as you willfully take on this endeavor? Do you know your museum's origin stories and where there are intersections with racism, other kinds of oppression, and ill-treatment of others or exclusion that continues to the present day? Have there been surprising and positive points in your museum's history that you want to commemorate over time that will help to remind you of your charge as an anti-oppressive space?

As you discuss your museum's past, present, and future in various meetings across the organization, various times during the museum's points of excitement and honor, boredom and criticism, and best practice and worst practice begin to formalize your museum's strategy. As you refine your thinking over time, critically observe what is happening in real time—how colleagues are responding to problems occurring in real time, being wise or helpful during complex interactions and answering questions about what the museum is planning to do about their DEAI provision.

Remember, it's not always about the new diversity wing of the museum, funded by the wealthiest benefactors in town. That might garner above-the-fold gravitas and thousands of likes on social media, but how well does that really move the individual needles toward social justice, anti-oppression, and healed hearts and minds? It might prop up the institution and reflect well on a donor or two, but it is not the kind of thoughtful anti-oppression aim that your DEAI approach is meant to address. Once the large building is erected and during the time it takes to be built, those who don't care to do the work to build community and change their behaviors will point to the massive construction and claim that their organization has chosen to prioritize this new initiative as a way to contribute to the anti-oppression question.

Led by your museum DEAI working group, sit in small groups of team members across the institution. Include options for write-in answers and remote calls into the activity. Plan enough time to discuss the participants' views of the museum, the groups' understanding of DEAI and anti-oppression as a major construct at the museum, and help each other commit to engaging critically in that work from here on.

A worksheet you can use to generate discussion and subsequently an internal values statement follows.

INTRADEPARTMENTAL DEAI TEAM PLANNING MODEL

Selecting and conducting an entire day or week for staff professional development particularly about DEAI is a necessity. The staff professional day rolls out the theoretical model, and the subsequent meetings throughout the year engage the practice.

Plan to hold a DEAI planning meeting once or twice a year.

During an annual start-of-year museum meeting, allow each department to spend time with every other department and give a brief report on the kind of work they do for the museum, the major activities on their annual roster, and the upcoming projects of the next few months or even years if known.

Someone from the senior staff/administration should then reiterate the museum's strategic plan and communicate that everyone should work according to their strengths under the advisement of their supervisors and using their power and desire for DEAI work.

The DEAI team, director, committee, or working group, including the board committee for diversity, equity, accessibility, and inclusion, should then present and explain how they will be assisting in providing their recommendations for DEAI-informed practices at the staff professional day and subsequent planning meetings as necessary, but they should reiterate that they value the input of all contributors. They should also create a plan for their own personal, peer, internal, and external community growth.

Each department should then share its vision and projects with every other department with a DEAI staff member or team member in place to answer and ask relevant questions. Some department partnerships and liaisons will be entirely obvious and familiar. Others might not seem as natural but can make for great synergies in the future. Some departments might need general, short-term plans with partnered departments, and others might require a careful plan over a year's time. The shared services/museum store or events department might need a shorter time to plan, while content- and context-heavy museums might be complex and, therefore, necessitate months or years, such as building and grounds, exhibition departments, and events or catering services. The museum's food service providers, exhibit preparators, volunteer staff, custodial workers, and others who may work on an ad hoc basis should also be included and be prepared to work alongside other museum workers and constituents insofar as they are able.

Museum culture is often a highly competitive one. Excessive competition and one-upmanship can be antithetical to the goals of an inclusive, decolonized organization. In that spirit, intradepartmental short- and long-term planning of core activities should be advantageous to a DEAI-focused approach.

Here is an example of an exhibition department's meeting with other departments in the museum to fulfill its plans over the course of a year. The ideal method is to work in person as far as possible but include other ways of connecting with staff members who are unable to meet on-site. Use this example to create your own co-departmental DEAI timelines and work plans.

EXHIBITION DEVELOPMENT TIMELINE

MONTH 1

The exhibition department conducts initial meetings between the curating and exhibition design departments to introduce preliminary concepts and establish shared goals and objectives. Team members invite members of the DEAI task force or committee to attend and foreground the need to embed thinking about DEAI in early interactions.

The exhibition department conducts brainstorming sessions to generate ideas for the exhibition, ensuring diverse perspectives and themes are considered. At this time, members of the exhibition department commit to being intentional about researching and identifying potential artists, artworks, or artifacts that align with the exhibition's focus on diversity and anti-racism. They also commit to sharing resources across the institution and across departments if those resources can be helpful in fulfilling other departmental DEAI imperatives.

MONTH 2

Members of the exhibition and curation departments collaborate on the selection of artworks or artifacts, prioritizing representation from diverse artists and cultures. They invite a few members of the education department to weigh in along with any community partners who have been involved with the museum and who know the cultural communities or identities whose inclusion is essential to the departments' goals.

Together, the museum team members engage in critical discussions to ensure the exhibition's narratives challenge and address systemic racism and inequality while considering other forms of oppression that intersect—both through the stories the exhibition tells and through the process itself. Decolonized processes will prioritize open dialogue, considering multiple viewpoints, valuing people who have different kinds of power and experience and who may lack organizational privilege, and fostering relationship building. The DEAI working group can help to promote team building, source writings, and other materials for personal education purposes as well as to include in the narratives and content of the exhibition.

The exhibition department begins developing an inclusive and accessible exhibition design plan, considering visitor flow, interactive elements, and interpretive materials. They consult with members of the DEAI team and physical facilities to ensure that building codes are up to standards, that ADA and ADAG standards don't conflict with the building codes, and that user experience agrees with what's on paper. If someone with a disability cannot access and have the opportunity to enjoy something that theoretically is made for them, it is a moot point.

MONTH 3

The exhibition and curatorial departments conduct research on inclusive exhibition design practices, accessibility guidelines, and anti-racist curatorial approaches. They continue to collaborate on the development of interpretive materials, ensuring they are inclusive and informative and challenge biases. They work with the education department to consider whether internal museum experts or experts outside of the museum can further advise or present in partnership.

The exhibition and curatorial departments continue exploring potential relationships with community organizations to ensure diverse perspectives and voices are included and to genuinely deepen associations.

MONTH 4

The fourth month of exhibition planning is a good time frame for solidifying the exhibition's narrative and theme and incorporating feedback from diverse stakeholders, including community representatives. They should start in earnest to collaborate on the design and layout of the exhibition space, enumerating and accounting for each main type of accessibility provision for individuals with disabilities and language barriers, acknowledging those with hearing loss or who are Deaf, those who are blind or have low vision, those with mobility disabilities, and those with cognitive disabilities. They may also wish to include artists, researchers, writers, and designers with disabilities as exhibition participants and contractors. They rely on the expertise of the physical facilities department and accessibility coordinator, and at this time, may be contacting community disability justice organizations to form focus groups as user experts.

In concert with the education department, they should start scheduling and planning related programs that promote diversity, equity, and inclusion, such as workshops, panel discussions, or performances. The communications and public relations departments should also be enjoined at this time to help source important calendar dates and avoid public event conflicts; begin to map out a media plan; and share information about the content, themes, and people involved in the exhibition.

The planning team should also work with the events department and physical facilities teams to make sure that the building locations chosen are available and free from barriers that would exclude people with disabilities and that there are adequate accessibility aids and loaner equipment in good working condition. It can often take months to source enough replacements or repair equipment.

MONTH 5

The department should establish a practice of conducting regular meetings to review progress; address challenges; and ensure alignment with diversity, equity, accessibility, inclusion, and anti-oppression goals. A member or members of the DEAI working group, task force, or committee should be assigned to the exhibition as a point person, researcher, or exhibition advisor depending on the nature and content of the exhibition and the most pressing DEAI concerns that need to be addressed.

Team members should collaborate on the development of interactive elements within the exhibition that encourage visitor engagement and reflection on social justice issues.

Include input from community members featured in the exhibition when consulting design and graphics and marketing and communications departments as you begin drafting inclusive and anti-racist exhibition texts, labels, and signage. An inclusive and culturally relevant design may include color families, typography, concepts of space, and sight lines that are different from what the department and museum are used to. For instance, the norms of bare white walls as backdrops or rectangular forms as pedestals could be challenged.

The DEAI working group can help underscore the need to be brave in attempting to present little-recognized cultural norms as legitimate, warranted, and worthy in the museum's space.

MONTH 6

The exhibition design having been finalized, allow other departments the opportunity to preview, comment, and acknowledge it, albeit with limited editing power, ensuring it reflects the principles of diversity, equity, accessibility, inclusion, and anti-racism. You may find that someone in the gift shop has good ideas that align with their concept of the shop's offerings to enhance the exhibition. This opportunity may be a brief staff meeting presentation or a short video clip. A key objective of this action would also be to promote collegiality and transparency, which is often lost in rushed exhibition planning endeavors.

Conduct accessibility audits of the exhibition space and make necessary adjustments to approach full accessibility for individuals with disabilities as far as you are aware. Remember that there are many kinds of disabilities, presenting in a multitude of ways, and that every person is an individual. You may choose to reinforce your exhibition accessibility provision with online and app-based support, partnering with disability service organizations to help with front-end evaluation by user experts with disabilities.

Continue refining interpretive materials to ensure they are inclusive and accurate and that they challenge biases.

MONTH 7

Work with the installation team to build the exhibition, ensuring that interactive and stationary elements are accessible, inclusive, and aligned with diversity and anti-oppressive principles. You may choose to eschew using materials that are not ethically sourced or choose to support workers from cultures or regions currently in crisis or under oppressive circumstances.

In the seventh month, you will also want to start conducting staff training sessions on diversity, equity, accessibility, and inclusion to ensure a welcoming visitor experience and to practice delivering content in equitable, inclusive ways. You should practice recognizing, interrupting, and mitigating microaggressions; choosing inclusive terms and language; and greeting visitors in ways that affirm their identities and personhood. Every staff member, team leader, executive leader, board member, volunteer, and intern should be invited to walk through the exhibition as well, with the express aim to contribute to the team's evaluation of the DEAI/anti-oppression-focused goals.

Begin promoting the exhibition through various channels, making sure to include the radio stations; bus interior ads and exterior banners; neighborhood magazines, newspapers, and newsletters; social media; and other avenues that might not have been typical in your past media plans.

MONTHS 8-12

The happy day has arrived! The exhibition is now open, and you have celebrated with staff, drop-ins, donors, museum members, artists, friends, casual visitors, advertisers, and benefactors. Try to use every interaction with those you have connected to to broaden your relationship. Instead of registering them as just a click on a handheld gadget, invite them to sign their name and leave comments in guest books, show up for related programming, give feedback online, and become members of the museum family in various ways—not just financially.

Monitor visitor feedback and engagement with the exhibition, adjusting as necessary to address any concerns or issues related to diversity, equity, accessibility, inclusion, and anti-oppression. Have conversations instead of jumping to conclusions when feedback is not clear.

Evaluate the exhibition's impact on visitors, staff, and the community, considering feedback to be valuable data and making good use of more traditional kinds of data related to diversity, equity, accessibility, inclusion, and anti-racism.

Hold both casual and formal meetups at the museum for internal staff and external community members to reflect on the exhibition development process, identifying successes, challenges, and areas for improvement in the future. Be sure to thank everyone who participated in the process and be creative but generous in how you acknowledge, credit, and attribute those who typically have little power or privilege in the sphere of their main work duties.

It is important to continually engage in critical self-reflection, seek feedback, and adapt practices to ensure ongoing commitment to diversity, equity, accessibility, inclusion, and anti-racism.

EXERCISE: CAN YOU SUGGEST YOUR OWN 12-MONTH TIMELINE FOR INTERDEPARTMENTAL DEAI PLANNING IN YOUR OWN DEPARTMENT?

1. Choose a major project that your department usually does for the museum and its constituents.
2. Enumerate the steps that are taken to successfully achieve this project according to your typical planning methods.
3. Review your steps and insert points along your timeline where you can invite personnel representing relevant communities and viewpoints to advise on significant content; in so doing you'll embrace new ideas and respect first-voice authority. Take special care not to unduly tire or stress colleagues; manage collaboration wisely.
4. Follow the steps above, in turn, as relevant for equity, accessibility, and inclusion.
5. Use the example of the exhibition interdepartmental DEAI planning process where helpful.
6. Share your individual ideas with your colleagues and start creating plans that reflect your combined input.

ACTIVITY TITLE: BREAKING THE MOLD: CHALLENGING TRADITIONS AND INNOVATING IN THE WORKPLACE

Objective: This activity aims to encourage participants to question traditional practices in their professional roles and explore innovative solutions. It is based on the story of a woman who cooked a meatloaf that was too big for the pan simply because it was a tradition passed down from her grandmother.

Materials needed: Flip chart or whiteboard, markers, sticky notes, pens

Activity steps:

1. Introduction (10 minutes): Begin by sharing the story of the woman and her meatloaf tradition. Read or summarize this story, emphasizing the idea

that nobody knew why the tradition existed but they did it anyway even it was inconvenient or wasteful.

A mother is making meatloaf with her teenage daughter, a ritual they've been doing together for years. As part of the tradition, each person cuts the end of her side of the meatloaf before putting it in the oven. One day, the teen asks, "Mom, why do we cut the ends off the meatloaf before we put it in the oven?"

Taken by surprise, the mom begins to think. She had no good reason other than that's how her own mother did it and that was the way she learned. Together, the two call Grandma.

"Grandma, why do we cut the ends off each side of the meatloaf before putting it in the oven?" Grandma chuckles and admits that she doesn't know the answer either. It was the way her own mother taught her.

Grandma's own mother lives in a nearby nursing home, so they all go to visit.

Upon hearing the question, the ninety-eight-year-old great-grandmother roars with laughter. "I have no idea why you are cutting the ends off the meatloaf! I used to do it only because I didn't have a big enough pan!"

WHAT IS YOUR MEATLOAF?

What are traditions you are upholding at the museum without any real reason for doing so?

1. Discuss the concept of "we've always done it this way" in the museum and how it can sometimes hinder progress and innovation.
2. Group Discussion (20 minutes): Divide participants into small groups and ask them to discuss examples of traditional practices in their work at the museum that may not be the most efficient or effective. Ask each group to write down these practices on sticky notes.
3. Challenge the Tradition (30 minutes): Ask each group to pick one traditional practice and brainstorm ways to innovate or improve it. Encourage them to think outside the box and consider how technology, new methodologies, or different perspectives could be applied.
4. Presentation (30 minutes): Have each group present their traditional practice and their proposed innovation. Encourage other participants to provide feedback, ask questions, and offer additional suggestions.
5. Reflection (20 minutes): As a whole group, discuss the potential benefits and challenges of challenging workplace traditions. Discuss how to foster a workplace culture that encourages innovation and continual improvement.
6. Conclusion (10 minutes): Wrap up the activity by emphasizing the importance of questioning tradition in the pursuit of innovation and efficiency. Encourage participants to take their new insights back to their roles and to be open to new ways of doing things.

7. Follow-up: After the activity, send a follow-up email encouraging participants to implement one of the innovations discussed during the session. Schedule a follow-up meeting in a month to discuss the progress and any challenges encountered.

15

Effective Ongoing DEAI Training

What does training mean in the context of diversity, equity, accessibility, and inclusion in a museum? What are museum practitioners expected to do that requires drills and coaching? On one hand, we all need to develop the skills of empathy and critical thinking that empower us to become more culturally aware of and responsive to each other. On the other hand, the word *training* brings to mind a regimented course yielding ever-increasing levels of high proficiency. It can be stressful and competitive to say we need to train to become anti-oppressive and empathetic. While there are rote elements to some of the things that are done with DEAI in mind, most often we are concerned with behaviors, cultural practices, patience, understanding, and welcoming stances. We do need to hear about how our everyday actions affect our peers, community members, identity groups, and those from whom we differ. We need to learn to become more compassionate and to listen more deeply for understanding. We also need to develop environments of more trust and less judgment.

I would recommend, instead, simply calling DEAI training what it should be: the work of everyday life, just engaging in the work. Skilled facilitators, consultants, and compassionate teachers can help you teach yourselves what needs to be done and should be called on if necessary. That said, listening to yourselves, communicating with vulnerability and intent, and focusing on your end goals should help considerably as you build these competencies day by day.

ESTABLISH A CULTURE OF RESPECT

Your primary value should be one of respect. As museum professionals, you should develop and communicate a clear code of conduct that emphasizes respect, inclusivity, and zero tolerance for harassment or discrimination. While it's likely that your employee handbook already contains specific sections on certain kinds of harassment and some kind of behavioral code, you should ensure that a specific section pertaining to respect and inclusivity and aligning with your DEAI initiative is clearly stated in the handbook. Nontolerance (zero tolerance) is not about being hypocritical. Not everything should be tolerated. We should be tolerant only to the point that someone's fist meets your face. Ensure that all staff members are aware of the expectations for and consequences of inappropriate behavior. Those with the most organizational power have the most responsibility, not the least, to be transparent, to be courageous leaders who model the most inclusive values, and to lead with compassion.

DIVERSE HIRING AND PROMOTION PRACTICE

Implement inclusive hiring practices that actively seek and affirm candidates from diverse racial and ethnic backgrounds, candidates with various differences from the majority of the museum employees' current makeup, and candidates who could bring necessary visibility to less well-represented groups and promote equal opportunities. Those you employ should be worthy of their hire, and as you seek to fulfill your DEAI aims, they should also contribute to your diversity and inclusion goals. Strategies such as blind hiring, placing job announcements in specific well-researched target areas, and asking the same questions of all candidates using a rubric can be helpful. Don't hire for fit; that's another way of admitting you are seeking to fill the position with people you already know and like. Hire for skill and work to help staff be engaging and inclusive enough that new hires will know they belong. Establish transparent promotion criteria and processes to ensure fairness and prevent bias.

PROFESSIONAL DEVELOPMENT AND TEAM BUILDING

Provide regular opportunities for formal learning about diversity, equity, accessibility, and inclusion for all staff members, including leadership. These workshops and meetings should address unconscious bias, cultural competency, and best-practice communication to foster a more inclusive and understanding workplace. Informal learning during peer shares, staff meetings, book clubs, and other interactions should be encouraged. Allow time for staff to accomplish these activities. Be playful. Let staff know that it's okay, even necessary, to relax. Get to know one another so that you begin to truly care about each other rather than only caring about how their work outputs intersect with yours.

EMPLOYEE RESOURCE GROUPS

Creating employee resource groups, or ERGs, can be a fantastic way to communicate to staff that you care about their individual identities, cultures, and backgrounds and support their need to build networks. It can be lonely to be among the few within a much larger majority especially when the field has never completely welcomed those who share your identities and culture. Take advantage of any intergenerational mentorship that can happen in these groups or among people who share the same cultural backgrounds. ERGs can also be ideal places for developing leadership skills. Members of your ERG may even wish to serve on the diversity task force, diversity committee, or diversity working group.

OPEN COMMUNICATION CHANNELS

Create a safe and open environment for staff to fully be their true selves without fear of ridicule, scorn, or shame. The museum workplace should be a place where everyone knows they can express their concerns, ideas, beliefs, and feedback in confidence. While no two ideas will be alike, they all should be equally heard except for ideas that give rise to hatred and harm.

If your museum has a human resources department, be sure to staff it with compassionate, kind people who will keep confidences, act swiftly to resolve concerns, and use anonymous reporting mechanisms for incidents of harassment or discrimination, ensuring that they are taken seriously and addressed promptly. If there is no human resources department, remind senior staff often that they are required to act fairly and without bias when deciding to admonish or award.

MENTORSHIP AND MUSEUM-SPECIFIC PROFESSIONAL DEVELOPMENT

As a champion of equity and inclusion efforts, your museum would do well to implement mentorship programs that pair more experienced staff members with emerging professionals, especially those from previously underrepresented backgrounds. Museums tend to consider these mentorship pairings—a longtime practice in introducing persons new to the field to a professional job—as internships or partners from outside the organization, where the paraprofessional is a person of color, a first-generation college graduate, or a person from another less well-represented group. As an inclusive practice, museum leaders should consider that their staff earning the least in compensation have little hope of vertical movement without additional support. Offer professional development opportunities, no matter their cultural background, to support career growth and advancement for all staff members.

INCLUSIVE POLICIES AND BENEFITS

Museum administrators should make a point of reviewing and updating policies periodically to ensure they are inclusive and support work-life balance, diversity, accessibility, and equity. They should consider different cultural practices, including religious cultural habits and mores. Museums should be careful about the so-called grooming and dress standards they sometimes inflict on staff. However, if someone wants to preserve their personhood, as is their right, or adhere to religious criteria by wearing tattoos, facial jewelry, hair coverings, lack of hair, the museum should welcome and affirm their choices. In terms of flexible work arrangements, the year 2020 was very instructive regarding how employees could step away from once-hallowed policies about certain sacrosanct in-person hours and bodily comportment and still serve clients, thrive, and find imaginative ways to keep the museum interesting. At the same time, those who absolutely need to be at the museum to protect the artifacts and personnel, work at the information booths, clean the buildings, and keep regular office hours should be remembered and thanked for doing a yeoman's service during very difficult times. They should not be left out of all-staff meetings or in-house parties just because they are expected to be at the front desk or with visitors. In the same way that museum staff found ways to improvise during the pandemic, they should improvise to acknowledge these employees and volunteers and allow respite where requested.

Museums should also revisit their family leave policies, making sure they are not unduly skewing the benefits in favor of families parented by a man and a woman. They should also ensure that bias is not allowing certain perks to be given to those who are already in favorable positions when other people could take advantage of cost savings and access to better health care. Another area in which some museums fail is the provision and accommodations for personnel and volunteers with disabilities. As Title III employers, museums know that they must provide access and accommodations for visitors with disabilities, but they sometimes forget that they have staff with disabilities too. A good idea might be to have a special section in the employee handbook and other employee areas online that help staff with disabilities navigate their work landscape in dignity and privacy.

REPRESENTATION IN EXHIBITIONS AND PROGRAMS

Museums should ensure that exhibitions, programs, and collections reflect diverse perspectives and voices—all exhibitions, programs, and collections and all the time. An occasional major exhibit here or there and small edits on exhibit labels will not avail much and will never solve the sweeping problems of lack of representation, inclusion, and cultural integration. If there is little diversity among your professional staff in the exhibition and curation departments, be sure to involve staff members from different backgrounds in the curatorial process to ensure inclusivity and avoid tokenism. Recognize all contributors to the museum exhibitions rather than only the star curators or exhibition team members. Allow space and time for intra-museum collaboration to occur in order to yield insightful, effective programs and displays. Make use of your diversity working group task force or committee as well. Remember the wisdom they have to bear and lean on them as powerful members of the museum team. When requesting the expertise of community members, please pay them for their time and trouble.

REGULAR EVALUATION AND ACCOUNTABILITY

Conduct regular evaluations of workplace culture, staff diversity metrics, and museum employee job satisfaction. Hold leadership and each other accountable for fostering an inclusive environment. Address any issues or concerns that arise in an expeditious fashion. Accept that many aspects of a DEAI initiative are affective and subjective in nature.

EXTERNAL PARTNERSHIPS AND COLLABORATIONS

Remember the "Nothing about us without us" maxim, a statement meant to remind us that if we are doing something with others in mind or attempting to speak for others, we should ensure they are in the room to shape the discussion and speak for themselves. This saying came about during the apartheid movement and over the years, became associated with people with disabilities as a motto for their needing to be included and not spoken for or over. If museums say they are going to be community focused, they should first get to know the communities they want to serve or have as partners. Find community partners with similar values and from whom you can also learn and gain insight. Engage with external organizations and communities to foster diversity, equity, and inclusion. Collaborate with community groups, artists, and scholars to ensure diverse perspectives are represented and respected. Make it a practice to meet the leaders of community organizations as well as the managers, coordinators, and people who frequent the sites and facilities. Open the museum facilities and spaces to members of the community to use as they will; find ways to encourage frequent visits to the museum so that community members will feel at home. Conduct town hall–style meetings, host lunches, and find other ways to turn casual meetings into deeper relationships that become friendships. Understand what they care about and how the museum can help.

BANNED BOOKS AND MUSEUMS: HOW MUSEUMS CAN WORK TOGETHER WITH COMMUNITY ORGANIZATIONS AND INDIVIDUALS TO COMBAT CENSORSHIP

In some communities, reduced intellectual freedom has an impact on children and on schools. As schools and libraries face book bans, museums can have a crucial role in their support. The following ideas are examples of how museums can help communities by preventing oppressive, inequitable practices from further marginalizing them.

CURATING EXHIBITIONS AND PROVIDING EDUCATIONAL PROGRAMS

Museums can create exhibitions that directly showcase the banned books themselves or elucidate their themes. In doing so, museums can promote open dialogue and help community members engage with the fears and misconceptions that cause some to prohibit the reading of these noteworthy works.

RESOURCE SHARING

Museums can partner with public libraries to offer materials related to the banned books to schools and community centers, visually enhancing or contextualizing programs the libraries are already capable of presenting. Materials available for exchange or co-presentations might include art carts, digital copies of the books, Braille books available at Libraries for the Blind, reading lists, or lesson plans. Museums make great settings for informal learning in clean, beautiful, safe surroundings. Museums can use their contacts and expert lists to convene stellar lineups of authors and critics who can serve as speakers on related topics or on the banned books themselves. Museums can be safe spaces for people with diametrically opposed ideals to engage in civil conversation.

COLLABORATIVE PROJECTS

Museums can engage in special projects with schools and community organizations to serve as partners in addressing curricular imperatives through the themes or ideas from the banned books. Museum personnel can visit the schools in an outreach-style experience that builds the capacity of both the school and the community center to present art installations, exhibitions, performances, and other initiatives that support interdisciplinary learning and critical thinking.

ADVOCACY

Museums are not neutral. Museums can stand on the side of those who are prevented from reading and responding to literature. Museum staff and leadership can join with individual community groups and individuals to demonstrate against censorship. They can speak out publicly against book bans and voice their support for schools facing challenges. Museums can use their platforms to raise awareness about the importance of intellectual freedom and censorship's deleterious effects.

PROFESSIONAL DEVELOPMENT

Offer professional development opportunities for teachers to learn about strategies for navigating book bans and promoting intellectual freedom in the classroom. This can include workshops, seminars, or conferences focused on censorship issues.

ONLINE RESOURCES

Develop online resources and tool kits that provide guidance and support for schools facing book bans. These resources can include information on legal rights, case studies, and strategies for addressing challenges related to censorship.

Part IV

Upward

16

A Beacon on a Hill

WHY MUSEUMS SHOULD BE STANDARD-BEARERS

Back to 2020, and I was hunkered down in my favorite office chair, nestled in an alcove between the piano and a wall with three framed paintings as interesting backdrops to provide the teleconferencing viewers a restful alternative to looking at my talking head. Work was plentiful and rewarding in the early weeks and months of COVID-19; I had worked as a museum DEAI consultant and specialist for a while by then and was funded by grants to travel and conduct weeks-long workshops and yearlong convenings in person in the years preceding the pandemic. When COVID-19 hit, the work continued, but instead of boarding a plane and hailing a cab to my destination, I crossed two thresholds and a rug, with a mug of coffee in one hand, laptop in the other, and a cat at my heels soon to jump onto my laptop; it was the easiest commute ever.

Everyone that year was sad, frustrated, angry, and bewildered. What now? What next? The general malaise that accompanied news of the pandemic, the mourning and fear over loved ones suffering from or lost to coronavirus, new working norms as folks sheltered at home, and the bald-faced murder of George Floyd with its attendant implications for civil and human rights drew out the deepest of emotions in everyone in my immediate sphere. As museum clients bared their souls, sharing their fears for themselves, their colleagues, and the field, it was clear that we shared the same emotional liminal space. They were vulnerable; I was vulnerable. They sought answers, but so did I. I never felt more humble. Teacher to pupil, client to advisor, I became friends and dear colleagues with a number of museum teams. We knew we were trauma bonding. We talked about trauma-informed learning and discussed what was occurring with staff who were either working from home or not working at all because of the stay-at-home model.

One of my newer clients that year, a museum in Brooklyn, was quickly becoming a favorite. We met most Fridays, and we held discussions that were grounded in contemporary art critique and branched out from the artists and makers to the problems to the solutions. We talked about DEAI, but we also didn't talk about it. We didn't need to; we dispensed with definitions and met each other where they were. I admired how casually they would talk about their work—not the work they would pick up when the dreadful coronavirus was finally over, but the continued work—their own reflections, their calls and meetups with their colleagues online, brainstorming, buying groceries to feed those in food deserts amid the pandemic. During one of our longer sessions, a team member who always called in from his vehicle sheepishly said he had to dip out earlier than normal so he could get the technical specifications right from his van because he was DJing that night for the neighborhood—a free block concert to buoy the community's spirits.

They planted gardens of flowers and food, delivered bag lunches, and made people happy with hip-hop music coming from a parked truck.

When I'm asked if I can think of and perhaps name museums who are Doing the Work, or who are successfully enacting principles of diversity, equity, accessibility, inclusion, and anti-oppression, my answer is said to be surprising.

I don't name the museums that swiftly and categorically dismiss members of their boards of trustees and executive directors in dramatic fashion to replace them with people of the global majority. I don't name museums whose capital campaigns fund multimillion-dollar buildings that they intend to fill with art and artifacts belonging to and created by Black and Brown people. I don't talk about museums that rename or rebrand themselves or their programs to appear more welcoming and hospitable.

I simply say that everyone starts from somewhere and that even those who are either praised or condemned publicly are doing some things right and some things wrong. It takes time to see the trajectory and to change people from the inside out.

When that change happens, it's indeed magical, and it's what DEAI can facilitate if done well. The long-term, systemic effects of successful DEAI practice will not be felt immediately and may not even be recognized by those among whom we work day by day. If it changes us; changes our relationships with our team members to be ones of compassion, empathy, and understanding; changes the way we work together to accept new ways of being that don't traumatize and oppress us; and invites us to work alongside our communities in love and friendship, that's a truly successful plan.

I think of a few of my clients who serve quietly and graciously in neighborhoods near their museums, the residents of which are not museum members or benefactors. I think of people who see museums as places of safety and offer their time and talents to meet that mission.

Few of these museums and their staff members make it to the national news or see their stories proliferate social media, and that's okay. These extended acts of kindness reflect on the individual actors and on their museums that allow them the time, resources, and materials to bless the lives of others.

After Hurricane Sandy hit in 2012, the American Museum of Natural History in New York City opened their doors to offer shelter to newly displaced individuals whose homes were ravaged by the storm. Similarly, the Field Museum has offered shelter and refuge during extreme weather in Chicago. This is not to say that these museums don't struggle daily to provide basic DEAI measures, because they do. We all do. We also need to allow grace and space as people and institutions learn, grow, and change over time.

A favorite children's poem from my elementary school days grounded me and connected me to humanity while it taught me French vocabulary, heightened my imagination, and called a little girl to civic and world action:

Je suis dans mon lit
Mon lit est dans ma chambre
Ma chambre est dans ma maison
Ma maison est dans ma rue
La rue est dans la ville
La ville est dans le pays
Le pays est sur la terre
La terre est dans la systeme solaire.

French to English Translation

I am in my bed
My bed is in my room
My room is in my house
My house is on my street
My street is in my town
My town is in my country
My country is on the earth
My earth is in the solar system

The words, as comforting to me as a meditative mantra, fit perfectly for me like nesting dolls, one inside the other, teaching me each time I uttered them silently that I was safe; I was loved. I also had a responsibility to let others know that they could be safe and loved with me and, thereby, seek order where there is sometimes chaos, seek understanding when none seems forthcoming.

Inward: Inside my home at night surrounded by those I loved but alone under covers with my thoughts, I rested comfortably knowing that I was safe. I was whole. I was happy with a family who loved me. We played together. We prayed together. We sang together. We had a strong family identity. I felt that grounding and protection. My parents would often talk to us about who we were as people, who our ancestors were, what their expectations were of us in the future. I had many questions, and I kept them inside. I was known to listen first and listen for a long time before I ever spoke, and when I did speak, my words were wise and important.

Outward: My mind moved to the roadways of my community. Sometimes I would walk to school. I'd pass the Moravian church, police station, library, and movie theater and take a shortcut through a bushy trail to the back of a housing development. Arriving at school, I met teachers, children, and others who cared about and befriended me. I'd express my appreciation and friendship in odd but unforgettable ways—writing them stories and poems, making art—the same things I do fifty years later.

Onward: I was three years old when my family flew from Kingston to Orlando for the first time to see Walt Disney World's Magical Kingdom, a new family fantasy theme park that had opened the previous year. It was more magical than any of us could imagine. Among my first happy memories are riding in the gigantic cups of the Mad Tea Party and seeing Dumbo the Flying Elephant, but above all was riding in a boat listening to characters singing about their small, beautiful world from their own perspectives. The *It's a Small World* ride was the attraction to end all attractions. Whirling windmills, cuckoo birds disappearing and reappearing, singing in full-throated glee about the world being so small and yet so large to throw its arms around all of us had me transfixed in wonder and admiration, its impact lasting throughout my life. If this could be called an immersive exhibit, Walt Disney World had me so immersed I was a convert. I was so thoroughly delighted and moved as only a three-year-old could be, but as a tenderhearted three-year-old who was already reading and was fascinated by culture, music, and art, I was positively enraptured.

Upward: The vicissitudes of life have a way of tearing us from our comfort zones and have us cowering for places to shelter in alternate universes. Over the decades as life started to not be as idyllic and perfect as Disney had described, I would come back to that happy place in my mind, recalling the words about peace, shared emotions and resources, and people of the globe thriving under the warmth of a single sun.

As of this writing, there are deeply troubling world conflicts and national struggles afoot. Spite, pettiness, and naked ambition masquerade as just rule while millions of common people pay the price in life and death. Again, the world wrestles with the question of how to heal humanity. Some pray in churches, mosques, and temples; some seek guidance from advisors, family, and close friends. Many count on art and nature to palliate a soul weary of war. They enter museums to find respite, to see beauty in a painter's composition, to commune with creativity, and to be reassured that humanity is not entirely broken. They come to museums to connect with others in dialogue about difficult questions with no easy solutions. They support, sustain, and seek museum culture because museums are safe and dependable stewards. A successful museum-wide initiative focusing on diversity, equity, accessibility, inclusion, and justice can communicate to internal and external audiences that they will be protected physically, mentally, and emotionally and that we are all in this together. Art trends appear and dissipate; the wonders of science can be supplanted by increasingly fascinating discoveries. History reinterpreted and recontextualized tells more nuanced and more illuminated stories. At each end, there are people seeking relevance, comfort, safety, and understanding.

Index

funding, 77
fundraisers, 58–59

Gallaudet University, 124
gender, 20
gender bias, 46
gender identity, 92
generational poverty, 121
generational trauma, 26; about racism, 113
gentrification, 115
Gift Shop, 57, 59
Glassdoor.com, 62
goals, 67, 94, 97; journals relation to, 15; justice as, 11–12, 55; in purpose statement, 131
Goodhart's Law, 8
Graphic Designer: in Exhibition Design and Development Department, 56; in Marketing and Communications Department, 57
guest services, 79
guilt, 25, 26

habits, relationships and, 16
halo bias, 47
harassment, 141–42
Harvard University, 28
hatred, 4; bias relation to, 27
heritage, understanding of, 23
heteronormativity, 92
hidden bias, 20, 63
hiring practices, 32; affinity bias in, 132; DEAI in, 77, 142
history, 116, 132; education and, 114–15; interpretation of, 117; of museums, 38; of racism, 112–13
history museums, 55
horns effect, 47
"How Racism Began a White-on-White Violence, May 2, 2018" (Menaken), 113
Human Resources Department, 26, 57, 96, 143
Hurricane Sandy, 151

"I, too, sing America" (McKay), 113
IAT. See Implicit Association Test

identities, 33; culture and, 61, 73; inclusive language and, 92; microaggressions relation to, 64; of staff, 121–22
ideologies, justice in, 83
IDI. See Intercultural Development Inventory
imagination, 35
Implicit Association Test (IAT), 28
imposter syndrome, 8
inclusion, 135, 144; compensation relation to, 121–22; of minorities, 81
inclusive language, 88–89, 90–91, 92, 126, 137; agreements for, 93
inclusive spaces, 32
informational power, 103
Initial Planning Phase, 58
intentions, in communication, 69
Intercultural Development Inventory (IDI), 78
intercultural language, 25
interns, 35
interpretation, 35; of history, 117
Interpretation Specialist, 56
introspection, 53
IT Specialist, 57

Jewish community, 3–4
Jim Crow laws, 116
John F. Kennedy Presidential Library and Museum, 93
journals, 14; bias relation to, 28; dialogue relation to, 67–68; exercises for, 15–20
judgment, 132; bias relation to, 27–28
junior employees, 10
justice: accessibility for, 127; Black, 19; empathy and, 67; as goal, 11–12, 55; in ideologies, 83; power and, 104; social, 17, 94; tolerance and, 79–80

King, Martin Luther, 104, 106

land acknowledgments, 76
language: for accessibility, 126; bias in, 31; inclusive, 88–89, 90–91, 92–93, 126, 137; intercultural, 25
Latinx people, 74
leaders: accountability and, 145; commitment of, 13; confidence in, 5;

culture and, 52, 101; DEAI relation to, 9–10, 20; on ethics committees, 81; privilege of, 8, 54
legitimate power, 102–3
Lighting Technician, 56
Linnaeus, Carl, 113
listening, 119, 132; respect relation to, 88; team-building activities for, 82
love, power and, 104
low-income backgrounds, 31

management: of conflict, 68–69; training for, 13
marginalization, 84; privilege and, 115
Marketing and Communications Department, 57
McIntosh, Peggy, 104–5
McKay, Claude, 113
meetings, 20, 53, 142; cultural norms for, 52; for ethics committees, 81–82; for feedback, 137–38; for plans, 129–30, 133
Membership Coordinator, 57
Menaken, Resmaa, 113
mentorship, 143
microaggressions, 13, 26, 65–66, 79; bias and, 28, 63–64, 71
Minneapolis, 3
minorities, 71; inclusion of, 81
miscegenation, 116
mission statement, 129–31
mobility, disabilities and, 126–27
museology, xi, 7; communication and, 35
Museum Guide/Docent, 57
Museum of Church History and Art, 58
Museum of the African Diaspora, 116
museums. *See specific topics*
music, 20

Naaman, 10–11
nationality, 19
National Museum of African American History and Culture, 116
Native Americans, 38; culture of, 74
niceness, 79
Noah, Trevor, 112
Noth, Chris, 6

Nothing About Us Without Us principle, 89, 145

Okun, Tema, 117–18
Old Slave Mart Museum, 116
Ongoing Support and Evaluation, 59
online resources, 146
open-door policy, of CEOs, 89
Operations and Facilities Department, 57
outreach, to community, 8
ownership, provenance and, 76

Park City, Utah, 6
patience, 75
patriarchy, 8, 10
peasant class, 113, 114
perfection, 51, 55
performative actions, 85
personalities, in workplaces, 63
philanthropic activities, 17
Pittsburgh, Squirrel Hill, 3–4
plans, for DEAI, 9–12; meetings for, 129–30, 133
policies, 33, 131, 143; open-door, 89; for repatriation, 76
politeness, 79
Portuguese language, 61, 69, 88
Portunhol language, 61, 88
poverty, generational, 121
power, 102–3; for change, 55; decision-making, 70, 77; love and, 104; privilege and, 33, 54, 101, 106–7; systemic racism and, 118
power brokers, relationships with, 55
power dynamics, bias and, 27
prejudice: bias relation to, 27–28; training about, 13
priorities, for funding, 77
privilege, 63, 113; exclusion and, 117; guilt and, 26; of leaders, 8, 54; marginalization and, 115; power and, 33, 54, 101, 106–7; training about, 13; white, 104–6
professional culture, 62, 146
professional development, 16, 68, 133, 142–43
Project Implicit, 28
pronouns, 92

systemic racism, 4-5, 106, 114-15, 134; power and, 118; slavery relation to, 110

team-building activities, 13; dialogue in, 68; Embarrassing Moment Sharing Circle and Reflection as, 70-71; for listening, 82. *See also* exercises
technology, 38, 60; accessibility relation to, 125
Technology Department, 57
thoughts, beliefs compared to, 34
Till, Emmett, 116
Title III organizations, Americans with Disabilities Act and, 124-25, 144
tokenism, 31; checklists relation to, 85
tolerance: justice and, 79-80; respect and, 80-81
tradition, 138-39
training, 13, 137, 141; in cultural competence, 101; cultural sensitivity, 77
transactional communication, 79
transatlantic slave trade, 19, 115; race relation to, 113-14
transparency, 12, 136; in communication, 77; in compensation, 121; for corrections, 53
trauma, 149-50; generational, 26, 113
trust, 11; empathy and, 63; inclusive language and, 89; of museums, 117; respect relation to, 87-88; among staff, 53
Truth, Sojourner, 118

understanding, 10; self-reflection for, 23
unfair pay structures, 121

United States, 37-39; Black people in, 116; disabilities in, 125; racism in, 112; slave trade in, 19, 26
US Equal Employer Opportunity Commission, 124
Utah, Park City, 6

violence, 4; of erasure, 118
visitors: compassion for, 24; rules for, 79-80
Visitor Services Department, 57
voices: representation and, 131; respect for, 54; in working groups, 12-13
volunteers, 9, 35

Walt Disney World's Magic Kingdom, 152
war, 152-53
West Indies, 74; slavery in, 113-14
wheelchairs, 126
white male majority, 37
white privilege, 104-6
white supremacy, 8, 105-6; colonization relation to, 119; culture of, 117-18
White Supremacy Culture (Okun), 117-18
Whitney Plantation, 116
women, recognition of, 32
THE WORK, xiii
working groups, 81, 132-33; accountability in, 52; voices in, 12-13
workplaces: colonization in, 62; personalities in, 63
workshops, 13, 53

xenophobia, 4

zones, of safety, 67
zoological gardens, 39
zoos, 55, 56

About the Author

Cecile Shellman's thirty-plus-year-long museum career and deep love for people and learning position her to be an advocate for individuals and communities that have been marginalized and less represented by museums. Her career has taken her from the mountains of Park City to institutions in Boston and New York, and in Western Pennsylvania, where she currently resides. She continues to work tirelessly in the service of museum practitioners, boards of trustees, and museum service organizations to teach best practices in anti-oppression and inclusion in the arts.

She loves her husband, Spencer; her cat, Fantasia; and the game of Scrabble, not necessarily in that order.